T0163350

Talk Thai

Ira Sukrungruang

Talk Thai

The Adventures of Buddhist Boy

University of Missouri Press
Columbia and London

Cataloging-in-Publication data available from the Library of Congress
ISBN 978-0-8262-1932-9

∞ This paper meets the requirements of the
American National Standard for Permanence of Paper
for Printed Library Materials, Z39.48, 1984.

Design and composition: Jennifer Cropp
Printing and binding: Thomson-Shore, Inc.
Typefaces: Minion, Abadi, and Apple Chancery

Disclaimer: Though this is a work of nonfiction, some names
have been changed to protect the identities of the characters.

for my mother and aunt

Contents

Acknowledgments

First: Thank you to all the writers who have inspired me and kept me up late at night; there are too many to list here. You have taught this immigrant son that all stories are important, and that the act of writing is an act that connects us to the world.

And thank you to Sara Davis, Clair Willcox, Tim Fox, Beth Chandler and all at the University of Missouri Press who have seen this book through to the end. Your constant faith in this memoir has meant everything to me.

I also want to thank the magazines and their editors that previously published versions of some of the chapters: *Another Chicago Magazine*, *Arts & Letters*, *Indiana Review*, *Land-Grant College Review*, *River Styx*, *Post Road*, *Water-Stone,* and *Sou'wester*.

And thank you to the New York Foundation for the Arts for their generous fellowship that helped me finish this book. And to my former institution, State University of New York Oswego, where I spent much time watching the snow gather on the shores of Lake Ontario and contemplating how lucky I was to spend six years among such nice people and wonderful students. And to the warmth of the faculty and students at University of South Florida for their continued support and encouragement.

I've written much of *Talk Thai* in various places across the country: *Arts & Letters* Writer's Conference in Milledgeville, Georgia; Writer's Colony at Dairy Hollow in Eureka Springs,

Arkansas; Blue Mountain Center in the Adirondacks; River's End Bookstore in Oswego, New York; my in-laws' in Savoy, Illinois, and Cedarburg, Wisconsin; and in Columbus, Ohio, home of one of my heroes, Jack Nicklaus.

And my thanks to an extraordinary group of readers: Carolyn Alessio, with her Zen-like wisdom; Dave Schuman, "We'll always have Blue Mountain"; Michael Capel, Nick Mazzeo, Mark Mazzoli, and K.C. Wolfe, my students and best friends, for all those late nights talking poetry and literature. And then there is Jon Chopan—my crazy, lanky, white brother—for his brutishness and moments of hyperactive wrestling. I owe you a steak dinner without the fancy stuff. Thanks to Maureen Stanton, my writing idol, whose kindness and absolute acuity is limitless. Loads of love to Stephen Kuusisto, my mentor, my guide, who continually challenged the limits of my thinking and motivated me during my darkest writing funks.

Pats and doggy treats to Ginger and Charlie and Savvy, my dogs, sleeping underneath my writing desk, who always barked their criticism.

My mother and Aunty Sue: *caup koon klup* for your permission. I understand now.

And finally, to Katie Riegel, my first reader, my best friend, my love. I owe you all that is green and alive and blossoming.

Talk Thai

Part One

Sometimes, while wandering,
when I cannot find which road
leads back the way I came,
the road goes anywhere,
and anywhere at all is home.

—Mus Soseki, translated by Sam Hamill

The White Elephant

My mother pointed to my heart. In me pumped the blood of a Siamese warrior, one who strode off to battle in honor of our country, in honor of Buddha. That warrior was fearless, ready to confront any danger, even first graders at Harnew Elementary. My mother touched my cheek. I possessed the skin of the warrior, she told me, soft and yellow, like the petals of a dahlia. She said I had sharp and keen warrior eyes, despite my bulky square glasses that were so heavy they often gave me headaches. My mother stuck out her tongue; we spoke a language the great elephants understood.

From her pocket, she pulled out a small Buddha. It was attached to a black string because metal against my skin gave me hives. I bowed my head and received the pendant in cupped hands. It was the weight of a wild strawberry. "This is a warrior's Buddha," she said in Thai. "Your Buddha." She looped the string around my neck. This Buddha had been in the family for years, passed down from generation to generation. It would keep me safe. It would protect me. When I wore it, I must keep it under my shirt. Never let it out in the open; never let it dangle freely.

Incense smoke swirled around me. I fought the urge to sneeze. My mother instructed me to hold the small pendant with my hands pressed together and repeat after her: *Phra*

Chao, please bless me on my first day of school. Please give me the power to excel beyond my abilities. I am forever indebted to you. *Satute.*

We bowed, touching our foreheads to the ground, three times, and then I watched my mother mouth a prayer. Her eyes were clamped so tightly the wrinkles around her temples deepened. When she opened them, she took a breath and leaned in to kiss the top of my forehead.

The Buddha lay cupped in my palm. I admired the gold around it. I couldn't make out his face, only the outline of his meditating body. I felt a strange surge of energy. My father wore six large pendants that clinked together when he walked. I had my first Buddha. I closed my fist around it.

This was how I understood the world: I am Thai. Thais are superior to any other race. Ask any Thai and he or she will politely admit to it. We will tell you that Thailand is the only country in Asia that has never been colonized. We will say there is no better cuisine on the planet, that no other country has a dish that can be salty, sour, sweet all at once; and our jasmine rice kicks the ass of all other races of rice. We will say our flag is red, white, and blue, too, but prettier. We will tell you that there are three things Thai people, universally, keep in our hearts: our country, Buddha, and the King. We will tell you that our King is the longest living head of state in the world and one of the greatest men to set foot on this earth. Disagree with us and risk execution.

I was born eleven days before the Bicentennial, in Chicago, during a time when the country was going ga-ga about being American. Among these proud people were scared Thai immigrants, living, at the time, in a small apartment in Irving Park, close enough to Lake Michigan to hear the waves. They were starting a Thai family eight thousand miles from their native home, and they were determined that this new baby, this Bicentennial baby, would be raised to be nothing else but Thai. "This is a Thai home," they said. "You are Thai."

My family—my mother, father, and Aunty Sue—moved into a bi-level in Oak Lawn, Illinois, a southwest suburb of Chicago, shortly after I was born. Here was Thailand with American conveniences. Here we were Thai. We spoke Thai, answered the phone with *sawasdee*. We ate Thai food, made with ingredients purchased at a Thai grocery store on the North Side. Bedtime stories were Thai—not "The Three Little Pigs," not "Little Red Riding Hood," but tales of Buddha defending us from monkey-faced demons.

So when Mrs. Savaggio—Mrs. S for short—called my name in the roll, hesitating before pronouncing it, bringing the attendance sheet close to the tip of her nose, a movement I would see many times in the years to come, my notion of the world changed. I rose from my chair, stood up straight, pressed my hands together, and bowed my head like a proper Thai student. In Sunday school, at temple, I greeted my *ajahn* in this manner. Why would this be any different?

I wanted to be the warrior my mother spoke of, wanted to stand the tallest and straightest, wanted to show my new teacher my abilities were far superior to everyone else's. But the silence in the classroom made my body crumple. I felt the cold of the Buddha my mother gave me against my chest, felt the way it pressed into me like a sharp pebble in a shoe. I sat back down. The class stared, white faces twisting in wonderment. Mrs. S smiled nervously. I looked down at my linked fingers.

When the school bell rang at three, my mother waited outside the gate with the other moms. She stood apart from them. She had come directly from work, wearing her nursing uniform. Aunty Sue waited in the Beetle down the block. When I came out, my mother waved. I ran to her crying because the day had been confusing and fast and she was not there—she, who up until then had always been there.

"Why are you crying?" she asked in Thai.

I grabbed onto my mother's waist.

"Big boys don't cry."

Mrs. S came from behind, and I sobbed harder because earlier in the day she had threatened the boy next to me with her "evil eye," saying she could see what he was doing even with her back turned. She looked like a witch, hair gray and frizzed, face gaunt as if she constantly sucked on a lemon. She patted my shoulder with a wrinkled hand and offered my mother the other one.

"Hello," my mother said too loudly. She shook the tip of Mrs. S's fingers.

"Ms. Suk," Mrs. S stuttered.

"Ah, call me Chin. Short for Chintana, hard name, I knowing that. You call me Chin." My mother rambled on without taking a breath. "We Thai. Yes, Thailand, not Taiwan, not Chinese. Ila, he good boy. I teach him math already. Knowing how to time. Ila, what eleven time two?"

I buried my face in my mother's hip.

"*Awna,*" she whispered, "*Ya kai keenah.*"

I didn't want to lose face in front of my first grade teacher like my mother had warned, but I could not make myself say *yesibsong*, twenty-two, even though it had been drummed over and over into my head, even though this was what my mother had been waiting for, an opportunity to show how brilliant her only son was.

Mrs. S tried to stop my mother. "I'm sure he knows—"

"Ila, twelve time twelve. We practicing every morning. Tell teacher."

I held on tighter.

"That's not necessary," Mrs. S said. "Please. Your son, he is a fine boy, I'm sure. It's just," she sucked in her top lip, trying to phrase what to say. "It's just he keeps folding his hands at me."

"Folding hand?" my mother asked.

Mrs. S put her hands together and bowed her head. "Like this," she said. "A Thai custom?"

My mother nodded. "We teaching him like this."

"He did this when I called his name in the roll," she said. "When I gave him his assignment, then too. When he returned after recess—"

"Ah, this Thai way," my mother said, understanding. "But this not Thai school."

"Right."

"I telling him no more. He will be good boy tomorrow. You see."

"He already is a good boy," said Mrs. S.

"Better boy." My mother smiled and pulled me away from her leg. "Say bye-bye to teacher."

I put my hands together and bowed my head.

"*Bab farang*," my mother said. White people style.

I waved. When we turned to walk away, Mrs. S said to our backs, "Does he speak any English?"

"Yes," my mother said without turning. "You teaching him more, OK?"

Number one question I get asked: How do you pronounce your last name?

Anglicized answer: SUKE-RUNG-RUNG. Repeat the rung.

Lazy answer: I don't. It hurts my tongue.

Smart-ass answer: Smith.

Number two question I get asked: What's with the name Ira?

My mother told me that she and my father waited till the last moment to give me a name. They did not plan beforehand, did not think what the sex of the baby might be. They had skipped ahead in time, worrying about how to afford a future home and move out of their small apartment, how to pay for the baby's college tuition, how to prevent America from stealing him straight from the crib. Thinking of a name was not on their list of priorities.

Often, in my twenties, I would have this conversation with my mother—the origins of Ira. Each time I asked, I expected to hear a different story, one with mystery and excitement. I want my mother to say she had an illicit affair with a rich Jewish doctor and I am their offspring. Or I was delivered in a cab during Chicago's rush hour, in the middle of a thunderstorm, and the driver was named Ira. The truth about my birth, however, my mother always reminds me: twenty-four hours of pain.

When I tell her the name is Hebrew, my mother says, "Is it?" When I tell her people assume I'm a Jewish lawyer, she says, "Lawyers make good money." When I ask her why not a Thai name, she says, "Too long." When I tell her she can't even pronounce my name correctly—Ira, not Ila—she laughs. When I ask her if she knows the meaning of my name, she says, "Means son."

In Hebrew, Ira means "The Watcher." I watched. I observed. I made mental notes of my differences. One: I didn't dress like other boys. My father decked me out in brown slacks and pink button-downs. My thick glasses made my eyes appear like those of a horse fly. I wore bulky square-toed gym shoes with striped laces while the other kids sported colorful Velcro sneakers.

Two: my hair was trimmed in the classic Thai schoolboy crew cut. Everyone else sported the shag.

Three: for lunch Aunty Sue packed my Muppets lunch box with fried rice, a hard-boiled egg, tiny packets of salt and pepper, plastic utensils, and coconut-flavored pop. As soon as I unwrapped the foil, the smell of garlic and soy sauce wafted into the room; some of the kids complained my lunch smelled like poo.

Four: the English I was used to was spoken by immigrants. Sentences without linking verbs: "We Thai." Unnecessary I-N-Gs: "I liking apple much." My family spoke with different stresses on words. Strawberry into stlaw-BER-ly. Casino into CA-sano. They confused similar sounding words, which often yielded great laughter, not at their mistake, but at the silliness of the English language. Atrophy and trophy. Or my favorite: civic and cervix.

Before school each morning, I chanted quietly: I am a warrior, I am a warrior. I put my Buddha in my mouth—an oral fixation that led to too much smoking in high school—and prayed to him, asking for a better day. I slipped into an alternate world. I am on top of an elephant—a warrior, a king—bursting through the wall of Mrs. S's classroom. With me are the animals of the world. I stand on my elephant, raise my arms up into the sky, and tell my classmates I am their new leader. Henceforth, I am not a crybaby. I do not talk funny; it is you who speak with an accent. At recess, I will not be pushed around. No more will I race Matt Menneghini, the fastest boy in class, and get slaughtered, because I can morph into a cheetah. Bob and Danny, Tanya and Tiffany will no longer stick rounded tongues at me. I will flash them mine, forked like a cobra's. Yes, this is how today will turn out. Much better than yesterday. Today I will be king.

As soon as I stepped out of the house, however, my built-up courage seeped out of me, and the strange invisible walls of this country closed in. I remembered watching a nature show about bees on PBS, remembered that if an alien bee mistakenly flew into a hive it was immediately terminated.

Most Thai immigrants viewed America only as a work-place. America provided jobs. America provided monetary success. America provided opportunities Thailand couldn't.

Yet America wasn't home. Home was across the ocean, over eight thousand miles away. Home was a panhandle country smaller than Texas. Home was where mosquitoes hummed exotic songs. My parents dreamt of their return. They talked of Thailand with such longing. In Thailand, they would say, the fruit was so sweet it made your tongue dance in your mouth. In Thailand, temples dotted the countryside like jeweled cities. In Thailand, geckos clung on window screens and chirped you to sleep. My mother often joked that she started packing for home as soon as she arrived in Chicago in 1968.

America secretly began invading our bi-level, seeping through cracks underneath doors, climbing through open windows, like an invasive vine that devoured houses in the South. I consumed television. I practiced my English by reciting lines from sitcoms and TV shows: "Here's Johnny"; "What you talkin' 'bout, Willis?"; "To the moon, Alice." I sat a foot away from the screen and sang commercial jingles. Oh, I wish I were an Oscar-Mayer wiener. That is what I'd truly like to be. Cause if I were an Oscar-Mayer wiener, everyone would be in love with me. (Incidentally, one of my favorite meals then was nuked Oscar-Mayer hot dogs over rice with a dash of fish sauce.) On TV, everyone was white. I never saw Thais. Never saw any Asians, for that matter, except for news anchors, and the news was boring.

One evening, I decided I wanted to become something I could never be, not in a million and a half years. I pondered this predicament at the kitchen table, twirling a noodle around in my bowl with chopsticks. In our house, laundry was my mother's business, like cooking was my aunt's. Aunty Sue prepared a bowl of noodles for my mother, who was upstairs putting away clothes. She ladled some broth over the noodles and sprinkled scallions on top. She then placed the steaming bowl on the kitchen table and sat across from me, staring.

"What's the matter?" she said in Thai.

I twirled the noodle round and round.

My aunt told me there should be no secrets between us. I could trust her with anything. I did trust my aunt, my second mother, more than anyone in the world.

I told my aunt I wanted to be white. I wanted to be a *farang.*

The bowl had gotten cold. My mother's footsteps creaked upstairs. I didn't want her to know this secret desire.

"Like Larry Bird?" Aunty Sue smiled.

I shook my head. Even though the Boston Celtics star had the sweetest release when he shot the basketball, he wasn't the white I imagined. I was beginning to categorize the different divisions of white. Larry was Sweaty White. Tom Selleck, my mother's secret crush, was Hairy White. Ronald Reagan was Boring White. Boy George was Scary White. The boys in my class were Wild White or Meany White or Stupid Fart Head White.

"Like who then?"

I wanted to be Ricky from *Silver Spoons,* a sitcom about a boy who comes to live with his enormously wealthy father. Ricky was blond, had deep, deep dimples, and lived in a mansion. It wasn't just the look, I wanted to tell my aunt, but the life. Ricky didn't have to speak Thai, didn't have to sing the Thai National Anthem every morning or have to go to temple for Sunday school. He was a white kid who faced white problems, which were, to me, simple, which resolved themselves in half an hour. Ricky was Perfect White.

I tapped on my bowl with my chopsticks.

Aunty Sue raised her chin and straightened herself in the kitchen chair, a posture I had become accustomed to; she was about to tell me a story.

Once, Aunty Sue said, she wanted to be like a girl in school. This girl had long hair with tiny bows in it, a fair complexion, and thin little wrists, which she put colorful bracelets around.

Aunty Sue was a bulky tomboy. She was often barefoot and found herself in fights, which she usually won. Despite this, she yearned for the life of that pretty girl. One day, my aunt decided to wear shoes with heels, put on her mother's long-haired wig, and applied her own makeup. I couldn't imagine my aunt in makeup or long hair, but then, Aunty Sue wanted to reinvent herself. The boys made fun of her new look, made kissy-kissy noises, kept pulling the wig off of her head. The old Sumon would have popped each of the boys in the nose. The new Sumon ignored them. After school, she gathered up her courage and went over to the girl and asked whether she could walk home with her. The girl laughed.

I never questioned the veracity of Aunty Sue's tale. I asked her what she did.

"*Choke nah*," she said. I punched her face.

I wasn't supposed to punch anyone, she told me. That was not the point. The point was this: to be someone else was to deny who you were and who you might become.

"Do you understand what I'm saying?" my aunt asked.

I nodded, but I was too young to completely grasp the moral, too young to understand what it meant to be an individual. I was an immigrant's son. What lay in the far distance was uncertainty. What I was certain of was tomorrow I would wake and go to Harnew and eat my lunch that smelled like poo and try to blend as best I could, and throughout that day, I craved Ricky's life, even while part of me wanted to punch him square in the face.

Wat Dhammaram, the Thai Buddhist temple of Chicago, was located in West Town, a community area three miles north of the Loop. It had been a Christian Church before it was converted into a temple. Garbage littered the street around the *wat*, and the smell of rot polluted the air in the neighborhood. Even though territorial markings stained the east wall—gang symbols spray-painted in multi-colors—no one bothered the *wat*.

When we arrived, Aunty Sue opened the trunk of the Beetle for the *kai yut sai,* Thai stuffed omelets, she planned to serve the teachers during lunch. My mother recited the same lecture on respect: I must be a good boy. An obedient one. One who respects her, my father, and Aunty Sue at all times. I come from a good family. Do not forget that.

My father fixed the wave of my hair, then ruffled it up again. He was always giddy when arriving at temple, anxious to talk to his doctor-friends. Though he was a tile chemist who made half of what they did, the *wat* was a place to unwind and socialize, a place where annual income didn't matter.

Upon entering, my family became a greeting machine. At temple, they seemed more relaxed, more confident. Out at a mall or grocery store, they would instruct me to stick close and be quiet, walking stiffly. Here, the rules were different. The *wat* was a simulated Thailand. I practiced speaking Thai with men in fancy suits and women in homemaker dresses, and at lunch, I'd eat papaya salad and Thai chicken prepared in the hallways of temple like an alley in Thailand.

I stuck close to my mother. She chatted with her friends, who were mostly nurses like her and Aunty Sue. From week to week, her conversations were the same: I read too much and now our house was full of needless Thai comics and storybooks; I learned math so quickly that it was hard for her to keep up with the lessons; in the morning, I sang the Thai National Anthem so loud she had to plug her ears. The women complimented her for raising a brilliant boy, a future doctor. My mother pretended she was modest. She shrugged and said she'd rather me learn how to wipe my own behind.

At nine, an electronic bell buzzed throughout the church, signifying the beginning of classes. Buddhism was first, followed by an hour sermon in the main steeple at eleven, then lunch, and finally language lessons. I held my mother's leg, but she peeled me off of her.

"Listen to Phra Ajahn, OK?"

I promised I'd listen to my monk-teacher. I dragged my backpack on the floor. Before I entered the classroom, I looked back one last time, hoping my mother would sweep me up in her arms and take me to get ice cream at Baskin Robbins, Cherries Jubilee, my favorite flavor. Instead, she just told me to keep going with her hand.

I turned and walked in. Simon was already there.

Simon was my Thai nemesis. I hated everything about him, hated his slim waist and fake smile that made him look angelic, hated the way he looked at me as if I was the gum he had just accidentally stepped on. My mother said I should try to be more like him. Look at how handsome and smart he was. Look at his life's aspirations to be a doctor. I wanted to be anything but a doctor. I wanted to be Superman and lift a car over my head and squash Simon.

I found my usual spot, as far from Simon as possible. It didn't take him long to start in.

"The mountain is here," he announced to the class. He made a fly with his fingers, buzzing it around his head, poking fun at my bulky body. It was to say that I was fat and the rest of the class were the size of flies.

I opened my notebook and began writing my name over and over.

Phra Ajahn Wangkran came in, and Simon quieted. The class rose in unison. We folded our hands and bowed our heads.

"*Sawasdee*, Phra Ajahn," we said.

He nodded and we sat back down.

Phra Ajahn had a bald head that made him look like ET and a dark mole that adorned the left side of his chin, like my father. He was my favorite of all the monks. Not because he played ping-pong with me after school, even though I hit the ball everywhere but the table. Not because we watched Chinese martial arts movies dubbed in Thai and clapped during the fight scenes. (In a fit of excitement, Phra Ajahn would rise from his chair and kick the air and make karate noises. Sometimes, his sandal flew across the room.) No, Phra Ajahn was my favorite because he called me Iyala, not Ira. The name sounded Thai, sounded important.

"But isn't his name Ira?" Simon interrupted, as Phra Ajahn took roll. "I mean, Phra Ajahn, you call him the wrong name all the time."

Soneteen! I wanted to say. Heel! Simon's real name was Polapat, but like most American-born Thai children, he had an American name also.

Phra Ajahn said, "You know what Iyala is?"

Simon whispered, "A mountain."

Phra Ajahn shifted his robe further up his right shoulder. He linked his hands behind him. "Iyala is elephant."

Immediately, Simon pointed at me. "You're an elephant."

The class erupted with laughter, but Phra Ajahn held up his hand and all was quiet.

"Iyala white elephant," said Phra Ajahn. "Very special. Sacred. White elephant there in creation of world. Born from the ocean of milk." He moved to a bookshelf and pulled out a leather-bound book. He pushed up his glasses and flipped through the pages. When he found what he was looking for, he passed the book around the class.

"The night before Buddha born," said Phra Ajahn, "Queen Mahamaya dream of white elephant. The white elephant bring her lotus. What lotus mean?"

"Knowledge and purity," someone said.

"Good," Phra Ajahn said. "The white elephant know Buddha

is purest. It know Buddha have much knowledge. It message from heaven."

When the book got to Simon, he quickly scanned the page. He looked at me, and then puffed out his cheeks. He passed the book down without taking a second glance.

"White elephant mean good luck. More white elephant in army mean army win war, mean strong kingdom. But there one special white elephant. Iyala. He save Siam from big loss against Burma. He have much *palung*."

"What is *palung?*" Simon blurted.

"Power," I said softly.

Phra Ajahn pushed his robe off his arm and made a muscle. "Iyala strong. Can fly. Still alive after four thousand year."

"I don't believe it," said Simon.

"Fly like Dumbo," another said.

"Ira is Dumbo," Simon said.

Phra Ajahn asked Simon, "Do you believe in Buddha?"

Simon said, "Yes."

"Have seen Buddha?"

"No," said Simon.

"But know Buddha exist."

"Yes," said Simon.

"Then if cannot see Buddha. Never meet Buddha. How you can believe?"

Simon shrugged.

"Iyala real. Buddha real. Iyala great mighty elephant. Big like house. Loud. Can hear for hundred of miles. When Burma kill all Siam solider, only king and elephant left, Iyala blow a wind through nose and push back Burma army, push back into mountain. Save kingdom of Siam. Iyala hero."

The book finally reached me. On the yellowing page was a drawing of an elephant, but unlike any I had ever seen. It had a great broad head. I had envisioned large floppy ears like Dumbo's, but this elephant's ears were small. On its back, a Siam soldier pointed a sword toward the sky. The elephant stood on its hind legs, and its long and curving tusks, its thick trunk shot for heaven.

It had defeated Burma. It was a hero. It was white.

Mrs. S spent an extra hour after school teaching me how to read. She wasn't the same after three. No more evil eye, not that she ever used it with me. She looked pretty, hovering over me, her breath a mix of tea and hard candy, as she pointed out lines from our reading textbook.

To read was one thing. To understand was another.

Reading was not like math. Math did not steer you wrong. Numbers were fixed. Language was an infuriating Rubik's Cube. At the same time I was learning English, I learned the Thai alphabet at temple, which had forty-four consonants and thirty-two vowels. Mrs. S never showed frustration. She simply smiled, encouraged me, and applauded when I did something right. She also wiped away my tears when I began to cry—which was often—because I couldn't spell a simple word like "monkey" or "hello." My mother, during our Thai lessons at home, said I was too smart. She said I understood everything so quickly she was running out of things to teach. But English I could not understand, and I thought it was a deficiency I would never overcome. I recognized that letters in a precise order formed words. I knew how to voice those words, like "cat" for example, knew that c-a-t spelled cat, but placed into a sentence among other words, suddenly everything lost meaning.

Once, Mrs. S made me do the sounds of the animals after I spelled the word correctly. C-O-W. Moo. D-O-G. Wuff-wuff. L-I-O-N. Roar. It was a fun game, and I tried to make the best animal noises. For the first time, I let down my guard to someone who was not a member of my family, who was white. Mrs. S complimented me on my spelling, which I was getting better and better at, and at my impersonations, she applauded and said, "I feel like I'm in a zoo." After I spelled rooster,

R-O-O-S-T-E-R, I made its sound. Acheee-ache-ache. This was how my mother said Thai roosters crowed to wake up the land. It sounded as if someone had a bone stuck in the throat. Mrs. S tilted her head, and then laughed, hiding her mouth in the crook of her arm. I laughed too, but didn't know why. When she calmed, she said, "American roosters go cockle-doodle-do. Do it with me." And for a few minutes, we sang to the mid-afternoon sun a language we both understood.

After a quarter's worth of work, words began to take shape. I don't remember how it happened. I don't think many people do. One day there was a gap in my brain, and next, my eyes scanned line after line, storybook after storybook. I enjoyed reading so much Mrs. S insisted I memorize poems and perform them for other classes, a way to help with my shyness. While my class worked on math, the one subject I excelled at, I went to other classes in Harnew Elementary, reciting my memorized poems, hands behind my back, as twenty-some eyes watched me fidget.

The poem I loved most, the one I practiced over and over, was "The Wind" by Christina Rossetti.

> Who has seen the wind?
> Neither I nor you;
> But when the leaves hang trembling,
> The wind is passing through.
>   Who has seen the wind?
> Neither you nor I;
> But when the trees bow down their heads
> The wind is passing by.

Afterward I made a blowing sound, a little whistle of wind.

Mrs. S taught me more than reading and reciting poems. She became a gateway into America, informing me about the ways of this country. I began to distinguish what was appropriate and when. With white people I do this. With Thais that.

"What do we say when someone gives us a gift?" she said.

"Thank you."

"Make sure your TH doesn't sound like an S."

I said "thank you" again, showing her how my tongue no longer peeked through my teeth.

"Silly boy," she laughed, patting my head.

Her tutoring propelled me from the lowest reading track to the highest by the end of the year. The next August, I was in second grade with a new teacher, and Mrs. S retired.

At home I was caught in Rossetti's wind. My mother posted The Rules on the refrigerator. In Thai, on a sheet torn from a yellow legal pad, The Rules hung in the same spot with the same daffodil magnet at the left corner for twenty years. Only after I graduated from college did my mother throw The Rules out and replace it with a picture of my dogs. At the bottom of The Rules was my messy signature—tall, uneven letters written in the hand of a four-year-old—a signature that meant I understood and would abide. Next to my name was my mother's perfect cursive.

The Rules:

1. Take off your shoes before entering this Thai house. Put your shoes away neatly so I don't trip and kill myself.
2. A Thai son should show the proper respect to his parents. Put your hands together. Bow your head. Say, *sawas dee krub.*
3. Never touch an elder's head no matter how soft you think it is. The head is sacred.
4. Pray to Buddha every night. Ask for money. Ask for success. Ask to be reincarnated with the same family.
5. Don't point your feet at Buddha.

6. Always speak Thai in the house.
7. Wake up at six like a good Thai boy.
8. Remember, you are Thai.

My father was my elephant. I was his rider. Bare-chested, he swayed back and forth on the bed, his Buddhas clattering against one another. He lunged forward, then backward. I told him faster, faster. *Rale! Rale!* We traveled only within the perimeters of the bed. Sometimes he nudged my mother, who playfully swatted at him. I wanted her to be an elephant too, but she said one elephant was enough.

I pulled on my father's hair, and with a laughing scream, we came to a stop. Our shadows danced on the light blue walls. The dark outline of my father's arm shot into the air where his nose was supposed to be. It was his trunk and he blew through it. I got off him and patted his head, pretending to feed him stalks of sugarcane.

"*Bab gum,*" my mother said, Sin. "Rule 3." She wiggled three fingers.

"Today, I'm an elephant," my father said in Thai, "not a person."

My father wasn't a person. He was a legend. I wanted to be like him, to talk and move like him. I wanted the streaks of white in his hair, his rough sandpaper face, his dark complexion like tree bark. I wanted his infectious laugh, that high-pitched cackle. I wanted his sneezes that shook the house and startled my mother and aunt into little peeps. I wanted everything.

In my pretend world, however, on the bed, my father was the greatest of all the white elephants and we were off to war against Burma. I said proudly, "Daddy is an elephant, my elephant, and he will follow only my command," in clear English.

"Talk Thai," my mother said. "Rule 6."

Rule 6 was the hardest one not to break. English was everywhere. It even began infecting my dreams—frogs croaking: "In fourteen hundred ninety-two Columbus sailed the ocean blue. Ribbbbitttt!"

"I like talking this way," I said. "I'm good at it. I hate speaking Thai."

My mother's lips thinned. She punished in two ways: an intense verbal barrage or silence.

My father slid toward the back of the bed. He, too, feared her anger.

"You hate speaking the language of your ancestors?" my mother said, her voice even and curt. "Then you hate me." She turned away, her eyes aimed at the dresser.

My father made his eyes bulge. He nodded toward my mother, a gesture that told me to apologize, to lay my hands on her lap and bow my head.

I couldn't stand her silence. It made my chest hurt and my fingers feel numb. I inched toward her. "*Khautode,*" I said. "*Khautode.*"

She ignored me.

I bowed my head onto her lap. I told her I'd speak Thai forever. I would never disobey her again. Never talk back.

In a cold voice, my mother said that only Americans were disobedient to their parents. "Are you American?"

I shook my head.

"Recite the rules," she said.

I did.

"Again," she said.

I did.

"Repeat the last one."

"I am Thai."

"Again."

"I am Thai."

"More."

"I am Thai. I am Thai. I am Thai. I am Thai."

She turned to me and lifted my chin. "Remember that."

My classmates' last names: Moritz, Soderstrum, Capca, Parsons, Tallon, Gilligan, Braun, Shinkus. I wished I had a simple last name, one you couldn't sing a Beach Boys tune to. The Suke-rung-rung-rung the Suke-rung-rung. Mr. Honkus, the gym teacher, did this every day. He also sang "Michelle, my belle" to Michelle Zekas—an awesome last name—and made her blush.

At recess, while I mulled over the name Ira Jones, I watched from the park bench as Leo Stankowsky counted to twenty so Mike Mancillas would get off the swing. That was the playground rule. You had till twenty.

Leo was a hyper kid with feet splayed in different directions. He had a thin head with thick black curls. He spoke with his entire body, hands spazzing all over the place. He ate pencil lead. I had watched him eat it once, cracking the tip of his pencil between his teeth and chewing it like hard candy. Then I watched him throw it up along with the oatmeal he had had for breakfast.

The lunch moms told us to count 1-Mississippi, 2-Mississippi, 3-Mississippi, but Leo counted so fast he did twenty in five seconds. Mike didn't get off the swing. He flew higher and higher, as if he was going to spin around in a complete circle.

Leo's legs were rooted to the ground, his hands moving like branches in a violent wind. "Get off. I counted to twenty."

Mike's feet scraped on the mulch under him. "No, you didn't."

"I counted to twenty and you're still on the swing and it's my turn."

Mike shook his head.

Leo grabbed Mike's leg and tried to yank him off. Mike held onto the chain, kicking and grunting, horizontal to the ground. When Mike let go, he fell with a thud, his shoulder hitting first, followed by the side of his head. Mike hopped up and popped Leo one in the mouth. I rose off the bench to get a better view.

Other kids in the playground began to gather around the fight. Leo turned redder and redder. I couldn't believe anyone could get that red. Then, with a war cry, Leo jumped onto Mike, wrapping his hands around Mike's throat, and bit him on the neck, a moment I believed Leo Stankowsky wished he had back, a moment that he would not live down. From that point on Leo Stankowsky was known as a biter.

One of the lunch moms broke the two up, a big woman who looked like a man. The girls made fun of her mustache. The lunch mom shook Leo until he stilled.

"Who started it?"

Both of them pointed at each other.

"Ira, who started the fight?" She singled me out—the quiet one, the harmless one—believing I was the one she could trust.

I didn't respond, but stared down at my shuffling feet.

"Did Mike start the fight?"

I shook my head.

"Did Leo bite him?"

I nodded.

"Settled."

She walked them off, one on each side of her.

The next day, Mike had a white bandage on his neck and Leo had detention for two weeks. At recess, Mike asked if he could sit next to me. He had a thick book that resembled an encyclopedia. I shrugged and scooted over.

"You have a weird last name," he said. "How do you say it?"

I said it out loud.

"It sounds like an alien's name. A Romulan one, like Mandukar."

I didn't have a clue that Romulan was an alien race in the show *Star Trek*. I thought the characters in *Star Trek* wore weird outfits and shot at things with phasers.

"Do you want to see something cool?" Mike placed the thick book on his lap. It was *The Guinness Book of World Records*. He flipped through pages of abnormal wonders. World's biggest bubble. World's biggest pumpkin. The smallest animal. Fattest and tallest man.

Mike snapped the book shut. He asked where I was from and I told him I lived on McVicker.

He shook his head and it looked as if it would come off like a top on a bottle. "I don't mean where you live now."

I told him Thailand.

"Do you have to wear a tie to live there?" he said and laughed. I laughed too because it was funny and because when Mike laughed he spit and that was funny too.

I told him where I was from was like an alien planet. I'd been to Thailand twice by then, and stayed in Bangkok, with my mother's younger sister. I told Mike about the temples with horned-nose giants, angels with peacock feathers. It was a world of glittering gold and bright jewels. When you were at a temple, you felt as if you were transported into another realm of existence, one that was better than first grade and Sunday school, better than Oak Lawn.

"Anything is better than Oak Lawn," Mike said.

We watched everyone play around us. There were two separate dimensions on the playground: one for those who ran and threw balls and laughed and sang, and one that existed on a bench.

Mike was my first friend, and we attracted another outcast, Kevin Cox, a lanky blond-haired boy with glasses that were thicker than mine. Kevin talked about fast cars: Porsche, Ferrari, and Lamborghini. Mike and I didn't care too much about that, but fantasized about spacecraft and black holes, interplanetary discoveries and time travel. We were friends despite our differences, and I loved Kevin because he had a large heart, which got him into trouble later in his life.

Mike and Kevin were all I could talk about at home. I told my mother Mike climbed trees like a monkey, and Kevin could run like lightning. I told her we shared our lunches because my two new friends didn't mind fried rice, and I didn't mind their ham sandwiches and Doritos. I told her Mike always wore these cool shoes, Converse All-Stars, and Kevin's dad dropped him off in a fancy car that made a lot of noise. I told her Kevin wore something around his neck, too, not a Buddha, but something. I told my mother everything about them because they were what made me the happiest at school, the happiest I had been in a long time. With my friends, we were picked on as a collective. The Dorks, they called us. The Three Stupids. The Poopfaces. Though we didn't like our social status, we had each other and cursed everyone else.

My mother worried. She wondered why I couldn't befriend any of the Thai boys at temple. I couldn't tell her that it was harder to be shunned by people of the same race, harder to take their name-calling and bullying, harder to know there was someone like Simon out in the world who simply didn't like you. I couldn't tell my mother that I didn't like Thai people, except for my family and the monks and the King, because being around Thais made me feel more like an outsider. I couldn't tell her the truth of what was going on in my life because I was seven and I had just learned to read and I was afraid of making her angry.

Aunty Sue and my father reassured my mother that having white friends was bound to happen. Still, she didn't allow me to go Kevin's house to play basketball or to Mike's to play on his Atari. When they called, she told them I wasn't home. When they came over, she told them I was studying. Weekends, we were at temple. Weekends, we were Thai.

I was walking home from school, humming "Beat It," by Michael Jackson. The weather was turning into spring. The trees had buds. I was a block from home. I remember feeling great, better than I had felt in a long time. I wanted to moonwalk.

I didn't think much of the three seventh graders walking toward me. My mind was on the homemade parachute I would make out of a napkin and some thread, which then I would attach to my He-Man action figure to see whether he'd survive a fall from the kitchen to the basement.

But these boys interrupted my thoughts. They crossed their arms and puffed out their chests, forming a thick wall. They towered over me, their bodies thick, faces dotted with acne. Even in the warm mid-afternoon sun, they wore leather and denim jackets with blue lightning streaked across the backs, and skulls with snakes slithering in and out of eye sockets.

"Where you going, gook?" one of them said.

"Jap fuck," said another.

These were the kids you were told to fear. Rumors circulated Harnew about them. They put a first grader through a car windshield because the kid didn't have the time when they asked for it; the kid didn't even know how to tell time. One of them had somehow died—really—and been brought back to life like Frankenstein with jolts of electricity. One of them had jumped off the roof of a four-story building just to see what would happen; he'd come out of it unscathed.

Further down the block, in between their bodies, my father's blue station wagon was still parked in the driveway. He hadn't gone to work yet. Worse yet, I could see my mother—my mother!—flipping through the mail, walking back to the house, oblivious. I wanted to scream to her, but my throat closed.

They circled me on all sides. I looked at their shoes. One had a hole in it, and I saw a toe.

"My dad said he should've killed all you fuckin' chinks."

These words—gook, chink, jap—bounced around my brain. I didn't know what they meant, and despite my situation, I liked the way they sounded. I was a boy enamored by sound, fascinated by the way the tongue moved to say a particular word. I often found myself saying a word over and over again just to hear it, to feel it. In my reading, I never saw gook, chink, jap. They weren't on the vocabulary lists the teacher gave us. What I understood, however, was that these words described me, and for that reason, I knew they weren't nice.

The boys began bumping me with their chests. I banged against one body, then the next, until someone pushed me onto the sidewalk. I crashed onto the concrete, my tailbone colliding with the pavement.

"I have candy," I said, which helped me out of trouble with the kids in my class.

They laughed. "Don't want gook candy."

There was a space in between their arms. I jumped up. Ran blindly. As hard as I could. They knocked me down again. Into someone's yard. Two of them knelt on my wrists. The other sat on my legs.

"Candy," I said.

"Pink belly on the Buddha belly," one of them said.

I tried to kick free, but they were too heavy.

They took turns slapping my stomach. I couldn't breathe. I tried to yell. Out came grunts. Moisture from the grass seeped into my jeans.

They slapped and slapped and slapped. I thought I'd die right there, my body in the position of struggle, my belly swollen and pink, my mouth wide open.

"Get the hell off my yard." An older man with dark bushy eyebrows rushed out of the house. In the neighborhood, he was known as the Greek, and for years after this incident, even through high school, he sat in front of his house and made sure no one walked on his lawn.

The boys let go of me, but because adrenaline surged through my body, I couldn't stop the flailing leg that connected with one of their chins.

"Fucker." He punched my stomach.

I threw up.

Before they ran off, the boy I kicked ripped off the Buddha pendant I had been wearing around my neck for nearly two years, the one I kept hidden under my clothes, the one that belonged to my mother's family, the one that made me a Siamese warrior. I stumbled around trying to get it back, but he, they, were far ahead.

"Are you all right?" the Greek said, more of a demand than a question. "Look at this. You tore up some grass."

I picked myself up and ran home. I had never been beaten up, never been held down. The physicality of it all I could tolerate. But my Buddha. I had lost my Buddha, and I feared, more than anything, disappointing my mother.

When I made it home, I vomited again. My father sat me up against his knees, and Aunty Sue fanned me with a newspaper.

"*Pen arai?*" my mother asked.

I told her everything. I told her when we played tag in gym, I was always It. I told her that sometimes I wanted to be white, and then sometimes I wanted to be Thai. I told her I really didn't know what I wanted at all. It gushed out of me. In both languages.

"What else?"

I told my mother the pendant had been taken. I waited for her scowl, her reprimand. She did none of this. Instead, she cupped my cheek and said in Thai, "Buddha will find you," and because my stomach hurt and I was dazed from the beating, I disregarded my mother's comments.

When I woke up the next morning, my Buddha sat on my bedside table, backlit by the neon glow of the alarm clock. He did find me. He roused from his deep meditation, climbed out of one of the bully's pockets, trekked across suburban lawns, avoided the canyon cracks of the sidewalks, hitched a ride on my neighbor's riding lawnmower, made himself into mist and drifted into the keyhole of the front door, and then climbed heavily knotted carpet strands up the stairs until he made it to my room.

That's what I liked to believe. But the truth: my mother had about twenty Buddha pendants, and when I lost one, there would always be another waiting.

In the days that followed, we began infusing English words into our speech. It became our little family language—half Thai, half English, my foot in both worlds.

My entire family was that way. Stuck, confused. All of them, particularly my mother, yearned for home—the familiar heat, the sweet mangoes, the monsoon rains—but also the safety and security associated with home, the knowledge that the next day would not be another obstacle. That was what we all yearned for: a sense of place, a guarantee of peace.

Under the Hand of Buddha

I always found Sunday-morning Masses on television fascinating. Before heading off to temple, I tuned into channel 32, enthralled by a man in blue-and-gray robes pounding his fists on a podium. He wore glasses, and his hair was bright white. He spoke unfamiliar words that sounded powerful: AWAKENING, SALVATION, SANCTUARY.

Upstairs my mother, father, and Aunty Sue got ready for temple. Their footsteps thudded from room to room. I knew exactly where my three parents were by the creaking of the floorboards. If I heard their rapid steps on the stairs, I'd quickly change the channel. I recognized what I was watching was wrong, but I didn't understand why. Still, there lingered a sense of guilt, of family betrayal, of Buddha frowning from his lotus pad, as this white-haired man spoke powerfully about DIVINITY.

Always above the preacher on TV were a wooden cross and a man draped on it. I'd seen the cross before—silver and glinting in the recess sun around the necks of some of the kids at school. But this man, he looked sick and frail, so thin you could see his ribs.

After a couple of weeks, obsessed with the man's identity, I decided to ask my mother. "Who's that man on the cross? I see him everywhere."

"Don't know what you talk about," she said.

I asked my father. "Do you know him?"

"Why ask stupid question?" he said.

I asked Aunty Sue. "Who is he?"

"Ask mama," she said.

At the bottom of the TV screen during sermons was always a phone number. I was nine and my mother finally allowed me to use the phone to call Mike and Kevin, but other numbers weren't permitted. She said she would know if I called anywhere else. It was her private magic. I was at the age, however, where my mother's magic didn't seem as potent as it used to, and I had become so curious that my thoughts continually went back to the man on the cross.

I picked up the phone and dialed. It rang twice before someone answered. A woman spoke so quickly I didn't understand what she said, a babble of words. I held the phone tight against my ear.

"Hi?" I said.

The woman cleared her throat. "How much would you like to contribute?" She sounded mechanical. "We accept donations of twenty dollars or more. With a forty-dollar contribution you get the Holy Book."

I had nothing to contribute. I wasn't sure if I knew what contribute meant.

"Hello?" the woman said. "What will be your donation?"

I quickly hung up.

"You're telling me, you don't know Jesus?" Mike sat on his bed, leaning against the wall, his math book propped open on his knees. It was the next day, and we worked on our homework in his room.

In the three years of our friendship, Mike had become one of those kids—different, a freethinker, and most of the time on another plane of existence. He was the smartest person I

knew, my best friend. We both read Stephen King novels, losing ourselves in stories of alternate realities, bloody murders, a
rabid dog, a killer car. And though I skimmed over the scariest
sections, Mike relished them.

I jotted the answer to ⅔ + ⅓. I was beginning to think that
Jesus was a Mattel toy everyone had but me.

"Who is he?" I said again, working on the next problem.

"He's, like, God's son," Mike said.

"Why does he look so sad?" Being God's son had to have
more benefits.

"Oh, I don't know." Mike put a finger to his chin. "Maybe it's
because he has nails in his hands and feet. Maybe because he's
wearing a crown of thorns."

I winced, curling my toes inside my shoes, clenching and
unclenching my hands.

The nails—this was new. I had been staring at the cross on
TV for weeks, but the image was never clear enough for me to
decipher that he was nailed to it. Or perhaps, the last thing on
my mind was someone nailing another human being to wood.
It sounded like one of Mike's crazy, imagined stories, an image
from a Stephen King novel.

"You're lying," I said.

"Am not." He rose out of his bed and jumped onto the floor,
slipping in tattered socks. He thundered down the stairs. A
moment later, he was back with a book.

"Here." He flipped to a page and pointed to a picture. I
crouched on his bed. Jesus' blood dripped from his hands and
feet, from the crown on his forehead, and from a wound in his
side. He wore a white cloth around his waist that billowed in
the breeze. Four men, a woman, and a sheep stood at the foot
of the cross.

"The Crucifixion," Mike said.

It was a wonderful word. I repeated it. Crucifixion.

"This guy here is Pontius Pilate," Mike explained. "He's the executioner. And this one is Martin Luther, I think."

"Isn't he black?"

"Not Martin Luther King. Martin Luther. And she's Mary, Jesus' mother."

"What about the sheep?"

"Lamb," Mike said. "They're gonna kill it for God."

I took it in—the picture, the cross, Jesus' glazed eyes, his parted mouth. My best friend had become a prophet. He was opening new doors in my life, doors my family never wanted opened. It didn't occur to me that Mike could be wrong, that Martin Luther came well after the Crucifixion. That perhaps it wasn't Pontius Pilate, and that the men could've been a few of the disciples. These were things I learned much later in college and they didn't matter then.

I stared at Mike. "Why are they executing Jesus?"

"Because he's dying for our sins."

Sins. *Gum* in Thai. I knew the word well.

"How do you know all this?"

"CCD," Mike said.

It sounded conspiratorial, like FBI, CIA, KFC.

"I hate it," he said.

"What is it?"

"Sunday school. It's where we learn all this stuff I don't really care about."

I thought of my Sundays at the *wat,* learning Thai and Buddhism in a small room filled with dusty books and portraits of Thailand. I despised it, despised Simon and the other Thai kids. In class, I often imagined Simon's head as a golf ball and I was about to tee off.

Mike's eyebrows perked up. He had two types of smiles—one was endearing, the other masked his mischievous nature. The latter took me ten years to learn.

"I ate Jesus," he said.

"No way."

"Everyone eats Jesus when they're seven."

In my imagination, I envisioned Mike and our fourth-grade class hunched over plates of Jesus steak, which resembled porterhouses at Mattson's on Cicero, my favorite American restaurant. I felt an overwhelming sadness for Jesus. First he's nailed to the cross, then you have to eat him. Does he have the worst life ever?

"Why do you eat him?"

"So he can be in you," Mike said, "like how Professor X can get into any mutant's brain and make him do whatever he wants."

Mike went back to his math homework. He asked what I got for number fifteen, but I was only on seven. Downstairs, his father's booming voice announced my mother was here to pick me up. I gathered my things and started for the door.

"Mike?" I said before I left.

"Huh?"

"What did Jesus taste like?"

He tapped the pencil on his math book. "A cracker."

Her name was Melissa, my first and only Thai crush. She was fifteen, a lot older than most of the students in my class, but she couldn't speak an ounce of Thai and seemed disenchanted with the world. Her Thai name was Ananya, but she demanded everyone call her Melissa, never responding to anything else. When she entered the room, I wanted to hide. I was afraid to look at her. Afraid my heart might explode.

I never said a word to Melissa. I was careful to sit at the other end of the room, so I could take tiny peeks at her and lose myself in her long black hair, her black clothes, her dark brown eyes. She never looked happy, not once. As each Sunday passed, I saw less and less of her because she rarely came to class.

The last time I saw Melissa, she stumbled in late and sat in the only seat available. Next to me. I pretended to take copious notes.

Phra Ajahn Wangkran was lecturing about Buddha and how people mistakenly compared him to God or Allah. These deities, he was saying, were just that, deities. They existed in the imaginations of those who followed them. Buddha, however, was a man who found a way to alleviate suffering in the world. He was real. Not a vapor or a booming, disembodied voice. He didn't have supernatural powers or grant wishes. He didn't create the world. Buddha's strength was his mind. He preached wisdom so that we could make the correct decisions to assuage our own suffering.

Melissa raised her hand. "What's wrong with putting your faith in something that may or may not exist if you truly believe it does?"

"Nothing wrong," said Phra Ajahn, "just not Buddhist way."

Melissa straightened in her seat. "Buddha teaches us logic, teaches us choice. But I find it comforting that there might be something that *isn't* explainable, something that governs us all. Something like God."

No one said a word. Some kept their eyes on the table or their hands. Some stared at Phra Ajahn, waiting for an answer. We had never heard anyone question Buddha, our Buddha. We had never heard anyone speak of God in our classes. But here was this fifteen-year-old girl casting doubt on our religion. I turned to look at her. Her forehead was wrinkled, her eyes red, as if she were about to cry.

"I don't know," she said quickly. "I want to believe I'm not alone. When something bad happens, like the *Challenger* exploding a few months ago, I want to believe there's something or someone to turn to other than ourselves. And I want to believe that those people who died are happy in heaven, or something like a heaven. I want that option too." Melissa sighed, her upper body collapsing into her chair.

Phra Ajahn took a step closer to Melissa. He smiled sympathetically. I believe if he could've touched her, he would have, perhaps placing a comforting hand over hers. But because he was a monk and monks were not supposed to touch women, all he could do was smile.

Melissa stood. She pressed her hands together and bowed. "I'm sorry," she said. "I don't mean any disrespect, Phra Ajahn, but I don't think I'll be back, at least not for a while."

Phra Ajahn nodded.

Melissa said thank-you and walked out of the room, leaving us in a disconcerting silence.

Later, I learned from my mother that Melissa's parents had enrolled her in Queen of Peace—an all-girls Catholic high school—because they were dissatisfied with the local public schools. They never thought religion would be a problem because they were devout Buddhists, preaching his doctrine to her daily. It was no wonder, said my mother, that poor Melissa was becoming "God people." She was among them most of the day. Her friends spoke of God often. He was everywhere in her world.

He was inescapable.

I was the only Buddhist in my fourth-grade class. I wasn't sure what it meant to be a Buddhist except every Sunday I went to temple and prayed in Pali, an ancient Sanskrit language I didn't understand. I folded my hands and recited the words I was taught. I kowtowed to a statue of Buddha three times after a prayer. For what?

The monks at the temple often spoke of the Five Precepts. The Five Precepts act as guidelines to a happy and peaceful life, much like Christianity's Ten Commandments.

1. Abstention from killing or harming living beings.
2. Abstention from stealing.
3. Abstention from improper sexual conduct.
4. Abstention from telling lies, from impolite speech, from setting people against each other, from gossiping, from backbiting.
5. Abstention from taking alcohol and harmful drugs.

These were rules that were higher than The Rules on the refrigerator door. Breaking one of these might affect what I became in the next life. If I lied, my mother would say, "Ah! Buddha make you insect next time. Small mouth can say nothing." If I stepped on an ant, she'd wrinkle her forehead and say, "Come back as hippo. Big feet. Small brain."

The purpose of the precepts is to give instruction on how to be an *Arahant,* a virtuous and humane living being, but to my mother they meant much more. If I followed all the precepts and prayed every day, in the next life, I would be reborn to the same family.

I saw Linus G. do the sign of the cross before a spelling test. His movements were swift and natural, like covering up a sneeze. He raised his right hand to his head, then to his chest, to each shoulder, and lastly, he brought his fingers to his lips and kissed them.

I began crossing myself, too. For everything. I crossed while crossing 95th during rush hour. I crossed before lunch and before playing a game of tag. I crossed before flying off a swing set. When the boys gathered at Harnew for our neighborhood football game, out came the cross.

I didn't mean for my mother to see the cross.

I don't remember why I did it or what I'd been doing when I did it; the gesture had become like waving.

"Why you doing that?" my mother said.

"Doing what?"

"That."

"What?"

"God thing."

I didn't know how to respond.

"You want to be with God people?"

I shook my head, but inside I wanted to go to CCD. I wanted to say all those S-words—SANCTIFIED, SALVATION, SANCTUARY, SAVED. I wanted the heaven my friends spoke of—houses on clouds, a place where if you wanted anything all you had to do was think about it and *voila!* I already thought about my heaven, a world that smelled of jasmine rice and meandering fish sauce rivers, a world of thundering white elephants and mythical Thai giants. In my heaven, I was an X-Man, best friends with Wolverine and Cyclops.

"I want to be in heaven," I said. I didn't meet my mother's eyes, but I felt the power of her gaze.

"No wanting to be born again with me and daddy?"

"I don't know."

"Don't know?"

"Yes," I said. I often found saying yes to my mother diffused conflict. Most of the time, my yeses meant I was on her side.

"Yes what? Be with God or be with family?"

"Yes," I said.

My mother's lips puckered in concentration. I could tell she was turning over the yeses in her head. Then she said, "You go be God people. I no care no more."

Later in the week, Aunty Sue dried her Thai chilies on cookie sheets, as my mother and I sat on the floor between the kitchen and front room and folded clothes. She had pretended to forget the cross incident, and I had pretended to forget how angry she was. This was how most of our conflicts were resolved.

I asked my mother, "Is Buddha like God?"

"Not like Charlton Heston movie," said Aunty Sue.

We had watched *The Ten Commandments,* and I had been wowed by the special effects. I told Mike and Kevin about it, but they already knew the story. The coming of the locusts. Parting the Red Sea. Moses and his stone tablets. It was in the Bible, they said. The Bible.

"But what makes Buddha different?" I put together a pair of socks, stuffing one sock into the other.

"Buddha tell us *we* finding own path," said Aunty Sue.

"We looking to him for guidance, not a—how you say?—," my mother searched for the right word.

"Sanctuary?" I said.

"Right."

I knew she didn't know what sanctuary meant, but she agreed anyway to prove she had a firm grasp of the English language. I had been amazed with the word, with all my new Christian words, and spent hours flipping through the crispy pages of our old *Webster's* for definitions.

I waited for my mother to ask me for the meaning of sanctuary.

"What mean, *sang-chu-a-wee?*"

"Holy protection. God is like a shelter."

"Exactly." She waved my underwear like a flag and placed it in the hamper.

"What about heaven?" I said. At temple, Phra Ajahn never spoke of heaven. I remembered, however, when I was four or five, heaven and hell were my bedtime stories. My mother said *sawan* was the place good boys ended up. *Narok* smelled of bad eggs and farts. If I were a bad boy I'd end up in *narok* where I'd transform into a crazy monkey, jumping like a monkey, talking like a monkey. Did I want to be an ugly monkey? In *sawan,* I'd be with Buddha and he'd make me into an angel, so I could fly higher than a bird. Did I want to fly? These were simple questions then.

Aunty Sue placed another sheet of chilies into the stove. "There is *sawan.*"

"But why do we need one? We'll just be reborn again, right?"

My mother tilted her head. "Heaven like airport."

Heaven: a rest stop before destination rebirth. I wondered if heaven had Chicago hot dogs, like Midway Airport, fifteen minutes from my house. I got hungry.

One thing still troubled me. "Who makes the decision of what plane we ride on? Who tells us where to go?"

"You decide," my mother said. "If good boy, be good thing. If bad, then bad thing."

I thought about how I accidentally peeked at Tanya's social studies test last week and how Mike and I burned ants with a magnifying glass and how I tattled on Andrea for putting gum in Jackie's hair and how I hit Kevin a little too hard and made him tear up. I did all of this in a week. For sure, I was going to be brought back as the worst thing I could imagine, the worst thing possible. An earthworm. One that fries and dries on the hot sidewalk. One that school kids try to split in half with their gym shoes. One that fishermen put long nasty hooks through.

I cringed at my sins.

My father was washing the Oldsmobile station wagon when a man walked up our driveway, two books in his right hand. My mother and aunt hung clothes on the line that ran from the railing at the back steps to my basketball hoop. It was a pleasant summer day and I tried to do a wheelie on my bike. I couldn't lift the front end off the ground.

The man said "hi" as he passed. He wore a brown wool suit even though the temperature was climbing into the nineties. He smiled, his face damp with sweat.

He approached my father, who stopped washing the hood. My mother and aunt watched from behind sheets. The man stuck out his hand, but my father showed him the suds on his.

"How are you, sir?" asked the man.

"Good," said my father.

"My name is Joseph." Joseph had a red beard, but the hair on his head was the color of tree bark; I wondered whether he dyed it.

Coming up the driveway in the same style wool suit was an Asian boy, no older than me, but much shorter. He stared at my bike as he passed.

"This is my son," said Joseph.

My father smiled at the boy, who stood straight like a soldier. How could this be his son? Joseph was white with cracked skin and his son had nearly the same complexion as me.

"You see, my son here, Elijah, his heathen parents abandoned him in Korea."

"He very handsome," my father said. "Looking very strong."

"That's nice of you to say," Joseph said. "Thank you." He told his son to thank my father.

"Thank you, sir," Elijah said, without a trace of an accent.

"We don't want to take too much of your time today, seeing it's beautiful and you are washing your car, but my son and I, we're going door to door spreading the word of God."

My father opened his mouth to speak, but Joseph cut my father off by raising his hand. "Let me ask you, sir, do you think you will go to heaven?"

My mother ducked behind the sheet, chuckling. Aunty Sue tried to hush her. I could see the faint outlines of their bodies through the sheer of the sheet.

"My family Buddhist." My father moved back to the car and picked up a frothy sponge.

"So were Elijah's biological parents," said Joseph solemnly, "and they left him for dead. Now, you are good people. I can see that. Your son here," he nodded at me on my bike. Elijah looked at me too and smiled. "Well, your son looks like a good boy. Aren't you?"

I stared at him.

"Yes, he looks good," said Joseph. "But Elijah's parents, they were Buddhist. My wife and I saved him from the orphanage where they fed him unmentionable things. Snakes."

I wanted to ask Elijah what a snake tasted like.

"Now, in chapter three of Genesis, the snake tricked Eve into eating the apple. And the snake is the Devil. So you see, they were feeding my son the Devil."

Joseph paused. His face grew redder. His temples were damp with beads of perspiration. Elijah stood still and quiet at his father's side. I noticed he was wearing Nike basketball shoes that my mother wouldn't buy me. I envied him. His wool suit, his shoes, his cool name. Elijah.

Finally my father said, "Very sorry to hear that."

"It was sad," Joseph said, shaking his head. Then he stopped and raised his chin high into the air. "But it was the power of God that saved my boy. The power of God that led my wife and I to that orphanage, the power of God that led us to Elijah." Joseph's voice got louder and louder. He raised his hand into the air like the TV preachers.

My father turned to look at my mother and aunt. He shrugged. My mother widened her eyes, telling him to get rid of Joseph. Aunty Sue hung up her nurse's uniform.

My father began washing the hood again in wide arcs. I believe he thought if he ignored Joseph, then Joseph would go away.

But Joseph didn't go. Elijah was still close to his side. "They are in hell now, Elijah's biological parents. They are paying for their sins. My wife and I spent three years in Korea trying to save their people." My father washed the side of the car. Joseph walked to the same side. Elijah followed. "Let me ask you something," Joseph said. "Where do you think your family will be after you leave this place?"

My father stared at Joseph. "Why leave? Good area. Nice school."

"You are a funny man, sir." Joseph laughed. "I meant where will you and your family be after you die?"

My mother walked toward Joseph and crossed her arms. "We Buddhist. We born again."

Joseph was surprised by my mother's entrance. I was surprised. To Joseph and Elijah, it must have appeared as if she materialized out of air. Joseph put a hand on Elijah's shoulder.

"There is no such thing as reincarnation. According to the New Testament, if you are not God's people you are doomed to an eternity in damnation."

Damnation. We didn't know the word. Joseph sighed, impatience creeping into his face. Elijah stared at my mother, as if she was a witch.

"Hell," Joseph said. "If you are not God's people you will go to hell."

In the silence that followed, Elijah looked at me and whispered *hell*. I stared right back and whispered *snake eater*. A few cars passed in front of our house. Aunty Sue shook a shirt and swung it over the line. My father and mother turned to each other and laughed. My mother covered her teeth. My father erupted, bracing himself on the car. I started laughing because my parents were laughing.

Joseph tried to speak over the commotion. "You can be saved. God has a big heart." No one listened. Frustrated, he thrust a book at my father, who took it in a soapy hand.

"Thank you for your time," Joseph said and turned around. Elijah stared at me again and mouthed *hell* once more before turning and mimicking his father's long strides.

When my father calmed down, he threw the book at my mother like it was a hot potato. She threw it to me. "You see," she said, "you see how God people so crazy?"

I kept the book, the Holy Bible, and later that evening I read it. There were numbers all along the sides and words like thou and thee and shalt and begat and compasseth and doth and sayest and hast and wherefore. And the names, names that tangled the tongue, some of them as long as Thai ones: Abel-bethmaachah, Zaphnathpaaneah, Mahershalalhashbaz. And the stories, they were confusing, enchanting, darkly entertaining. As I read, I imagined the Bible unfolded in comic book panels. In this panel, a slimy snake curls around Eve's long, bare leg and convinces her to take a bite of the apple, which sparkles on the Tree of the Knowledge of Good and Evil. The snake even winks. In another panel, Cain, face hidden in shadow, confronts Abel for the last time. We don't witness the murder, but we see the word THWACK!

But I had questions. Many. Why two creation stories? In chapter one, God created everything and then he created man and woman together. In the second chapter, there was another creation story. Here God created man, Adam, and then all the animals which Adam named, then Eve from Adam's rib. Why couldn't the writer pick one story?

And geez, God could be a mean dude. He favored Abel's offering of sheep. He destroyed cities. He told Abraham to kill his son. I wondered whether people prayed to God out of fear.

"Mike, do you fear God?"

"You're supposed to."

Recess again, and we chilled on the bench where we first met. Kevin was crouched down at the fence looking at Beth, the girl he loved, hopscotching. He was the first of us to proclaim a crush.

"I've been reading the Bible," I said, "and if I was Christian, I'd be scared of God. I'd be scared every second of the day."

"I don't believe in him."

"What do you believe in?"

"Nothing."

"How can you believe in nothing?"

"I believe in something, I guess. But I don't believe in stories. In a guy who thinks he's badass and can blow up cities."

"Sodom and Gomorrah?" I said.

"Yep," Mike said.

Kevin sighed because Beth was hopping.

"Do you know what God told Job after he killed his crops, killed his family, and made Job look like Freddy Krueger?"

I shook my head.

"He says, 'I am God. Never question me or I'll kill you.'"

The lunch mom blew the whistle that signified the end of recess. Kevin jumped up and raced to the front of the line so he could stand behind Beth. Mike got off the bench. I stood where I was, thinking about Freddy Krueger, my family dead. I stood there so long I hadn't realized Mike was calling my name, telling me to hurry, telling me to forget about God because if we didn't get in line we'd get detention and then we'd have to face our parents and no god, no matter his power, could help us then.

Religion bounced around in my head. The more I learned, the more confused I became. Was God evil or not? Why was Buddha fat in some countries and skinny in others? Nothing made sense. Nothing seemed to fit. Religions were theories with holes, puzzles lacking essential pieces. I began to feel, perhaps, the same suffocating confusion as Melissa did, and I understood why she had left the *wat*.

Though I couldn't quite grasp Buddhism or Christianity, I found myself becoming more obsessed with certain aspects of each.

With Christianity, it was exactly what Melissa had spoken about—the notion of a constant companion. I decided my God wasn't an angry man. He was just one of the guys, like Mike and Kevin. He became an imaginary friend. Each night after I said my prayers in homage to Buddha, I spoke to God. I'd say, "God, how are you?" I would tell God about my day—Boy Scouts and gym classes, my secret crush on Kristin, the new girl down the block. God listened. Sometimes he talked back. He sounded like my principal, a man with a voice that dwelled in the guts. Because I couldn't see God, I made Charlie, my teddy bear, the embodiment of him. It was easier to talk to something than to talk to air.

I would say to God, "What creation story is true?"

"What do you think?" said God.

"I don't know."

"Well, there you go," said God.

Or: "So, Mike said he ate you and you tasted like a cracker."

"I guess I do," said God.

"I hate crackers. I like rice."

He was there. Always. Or at least when my imagination allowed him to be. I found comfort in that, especially when the shadows deepened at night, when part of my mind saw moving monsters in the closet or my ears imagined creaking chairs. The mere knowledge of him watching over me gave me a sense of peace, of relief.

With Buddhism, I clung to Buddha himself. His image. I spent hours in front of the Buddha in our living room, drawing his figure in a sketchbook. I drew him from different angles and perspectives. I drew close-ups of his face, his serene, half-open eyes, his slight smile. I focused in on his hands, smooth on his lap. When my mother and aunt visited their friends, I asked to be excused so I could draw their Buddhas. They thought I was a special child, a Buddha child. I became the ideal Buddhist youth, an example to other Thai children. "You see Ira, you see how he loves Buddha." I played the role occasionally, enjoying the attention. When someone sneezed, I said, "Buddha Bless." In a moment of frustration, it was not "Oh God"; it was "Oh Buddha."

I carried my notebook everywhere I went. Stopped and sketched every Buddha I passed. The fat ones in Chinatown, the anorexic looking Buddha in our Thai textbook, the red-lipped Buddha at the Korean restaurant. I drew and drew and drew. It wasn't because I was a devout Buddhist. It was because I wasn't. I wanted to capture in my drawings the Buddhism I wasn't seeing, the lessons not spoken or preached. The more I drew, the more I hoped an answer would fall like the gravity apple that hit Isaac, and there it would be, spelled out in a language I understood: the reason why I was a Buddhist.

In early spring my mother's friend's son passed away. He had been driving too quickly around a curve on Lake Shore Drive. They held a service at the temple for him. I didn't want to go but agreed to keep my mother company. She had been crying all night for the death of this boy, even though she barely knew him. I had never seen my mother cry before.

I wore jeans and a T-shirt and sat in the back of the temple, my Buddha sketchbook tucked under my arm. The most venerable of the monks, the Chaoawad, prepared the holy water by melting a yellow candle into an ornate copper bowl shaped like a lotus bud. At the front of the temple was Buddha. He loomed above us, about ten feet high and ten feet wide. This Buddha appeared more alert, more awake than most Buddhas.

There were only a handful of people attending the service, mostly women dressed in black. When the monks started praying, everyone folded their hands together and closed their eyes. The room hummed and buzzed, bassy voices echoing off walls.

I opened my notebook and began to draw. I drew the delicate curve of Buddha's nose, and tried to capture his oval chin. He sat in perfect posture; his torso was in the shape of a V. Buddha's earlobes nearly touched his shoulders, a sign of wisdom. But what my eyes kept drifting to were the positions of his hands, smooth and gracefully arched, like a breaching whale. One bubbled up a bit, as if there was something underneath it, as if he were concealing a secret. I drew that hand over and over. I focused hard on it, squinting.

I had concentrated so hard on my drawing I hadn't noticed the service was over. My mother said it was time to go, but I asked her if I could stay a moment longer. Of course, she said, and took a seat next to me, draping her arm around my shoulder. She took a quick glance at my notebook and said, "So pretty." Then she kissed the top of my head.

Her presence was a comfort, but I was drifting off. I was losing some connection to the talking and walking world, and felt as if I was flying toward the Buddha at the front of the temple, flying and becoming smaller and smaller until I was the size of a sparrow. It was a surreal sensation I can compare to only once when I had eaten too much spicy food in a Thai restaurant in St. Louis to impress my future wife, the sizzling pain becoming a pleasant euphoric trance. But what I was feeling then, or imagined feeling, seemed spiritual and beyond comprehension.

The miniature me stood in Buddha's golden lap. He climbed down one of Buddha's long fingers and peeked at what lay under Buddha's hand. He saw something, an undecipherable shape. It was covered in darkness.

My mother nudged me. I was back in my seat. The Chaoawad stood beside her. She instructed me to pay my respect, and I stood quickly and folded my hands together, forgetting about the pencil until it nearly stabbed my eye.

"I see you back here drawing fast," he said. "Drawing what?"

My mother spoke for me. "Buddha," she said in Thai. "He's been drawing Buddha all this time."

The Chaoawad tilted his shaved head. His entire body was covered in earthy orange robes. He was shorter than even my mother and bone thin. I couldn't see his hands. The only uncovered parts of him were his head and feet. Under his thick glasses that took up half his face, his eyes were soft. He reminded me of Yoda from the movie *Star Wars,* the ancient Jedi master.

"May I see?" he said.

I handed my notebook to him.

He flipped through the pages of my sketches, pausing longer on some. I wasn't an artist. I knew my drawings weren't perfect—Buddha's eyes were monstrous in some pictures and his head too big for his body in others. Some I erased so hard I tore the page. But these were my private drawings, my vision of Buddhism on a given day, time, or hour. I was afraid the Chaoawad would think I was a sinner, drawing our Buddha imperfectly.

He opened the sketchbook to the Buddha I had been drawing that evening. "You see Phra Chao with different eye. Draw what is not there. But more here." He pointed to my heart. "That is Buddha way."

I don't see anything, I wanted to say. My drawings were crummy searches for something I didn't understand. I wanted to tell him I spoke to God sometimes and that made me feel OK, not sinful, not like I had done something wrong. I wanted to ask him about what might be under Buddha's hand, if anything at all.

The Chaoawad handed back my sketchbook and before I took it from him I put my hands together and bowed my head.

"Good boy," he said. "Smart boy." He turned and left the room.

I sat back down and stared at Buddha, hoping for the moment to come back.

My mother, father, and I were on our way to Holland, Michigan, for the yearly Tulip Time Festival. Mrs. Wilson, my fourth-grade teacher, said it was the most beautiful event she had ever been to—the parade, windmills, and millions of blooming tulips. She'd said it was as if you had stepped through a portal and had been transported to the Netherlands.

On the way to Holland, we passed two dogs in the middle of the median on Ridgeland Avenue, twenty minutes from our house. One dog lay dead, the other walked in circles around its companion. The one that was alive had dark brown fur with white patches. It walked, lay down, nuzzling its friend, and then got up to walk again. Its steps were frantic, jumpy, as if at any moment it expected the other dog to leap up and then they'd be off to wherever it was they were heading.

My mother said, "*Tow, tow.*" Poor thing, poor thing. We were in the lane closest to the median, so my father slowed down, careful not to scare the dog, and when we were past it, he sped up.

My mother folded her hands and whispered a quick prayer. My father closed his eyes briefly and shook his head. He looked at me in the rearview mirror.

"It's OK," he said.

"In heaven," said my mother, her voice soft.

I couldn't keep it in any longer, but I didn't make a sound. I wiped at my face quickly. Heat rose in my cheeks. I sat and cried for the next hour.

When we arrived in Holland, my father yanked us from store to store, buying me everything: fudge, ice cream, lollipops, corn dogs, fried dough. We found a place to sit and watched the parade go by. The local high school band blared on trumpets, tubas, and flutes. It was easy to forget. We were trying hard to.

In the early evening, before we started back toward Chicago, we walked through Veldheer Tulip Gardens. The sun was setting, and the sky and clouds were an amalgam of reds, pinks, and oranges. We were surrounded by tulips—rows and rows of infinite blooms like millions of colorful tears.

I was between my parents. I asked my mother whether dogs were reborn.

"Of course," she said.

"Everything," said my father.

"Do you think it's happier?" I asked.

"Yes," said my mother.

My father told me that dogs were one of the noblest animals in the world. When they died they came back as something or someone of importance. A king, a warrior, a monk.

I jogged on ahead, passing the darkest purples, the lightest lavenders. When I turned to see where my parents were, they were backlit and in silhouette, far behind, hands linked, my mother laughing into the sky. That moment was the most intimate I would ever see my parents.

As I watched them that spring evening, I thought about heaven, and if there was one, I would want it to look like this: a world of tulips, sprouting in every corner, the sky forever a painter's palette. And I would have my mother and father there with me, holding hands, laughing and loving each other.

And if I was reincarnated, I wanted to be a tulip, petals spread wide like a cup ready to catch rain, a yellow tulip, bright like the shine of a Buddha, and my mother and father could be the nurturing earth that housed the bulb, or maybe they would be the sun that willed the tulip out of the ground and into the light.

A World of Adjusters

Aunty Sue was the master of the kitchen, a black belt in culinary creativity. Over the years she concocted miracles, a combination of intuition and imagination, making use of the ingredients this country had to offer. A taste of Thailand in Oak Lawn, Illinois.

I saw the effect her food had on my mother, the sheer delight that played over her face. Whenever she indulged in my aunt's spicy curry stew—her favorite—she closed her eyes as if anticipating a kiss, and I knew she wasn't in our kitchen anymore. Where she had gone, mynahs jabbered like frantic schoolgirls and a dusty dog trotted under the shade of a banana tree. That was the power of Aunty Sue's cooking. It brought to my mother the familiarities of her life in Thailand.

When I was six or seven, I took on the role of her apprentice, mimicking her every move. I cooked alongside my aunt. In a plastic bowl, I mixed my Star Wars action figures with a spatula, tossing Chewy and Han in the air. At the stove my aunt cooked the Sunday dinner, Phad Thai, the national dish of Thailand.

My mother sewed in the other room. The sound of her Singer blended into the symphony of sound from my aunt's kitchen. My father watched the final round of a golf tournament downstairs, while putting at a masking-tape X on the carpet.

The smell of fried garlic floated through the house. Aunty Sue asked if I could close all the bedroom doors and closets. She didn't want our clothes and bedding to smell like dinner. I didn't mind—I wanted the world to smell like garlic and fish sauce. I did what she asked anyway, providing she kept an eye on my *Star Wars* meal.

When I came back, I watched my aunt chopstick a noodle and taste it. She thought while she chewed, her forehead etched in deep concentration. I picked up Princess Leah and nibbled on her plastic head.

"More *manow*," she mumbled. Lime.

"Mine, too," I said in Thai.

She squeezed a sliver of lime and handed me what was left. The wok sizzled.

I squeezed as hard as I could to get a drop or two. I threw in grapes and poured milk over the cast of *Star Wars*. My aunt occasionally winked at me. "*Aroy, chimai?*" she asked. It's going to be delicious, isn't it?

I dipped my finger in the mix. "Yes," I said.

After ten minutes, my aunt banged on the wok, a dull chime that informed my mother and father dinner was ready.

We sat around the table, Phad Thai steaming in front of us.

My mother ate hers with extra sugar and bean sprouts. No shrimp. She liked her noodles overcooked until they stuck together, soft and impossible to chopstick. My Phad Thai had more egg and shrimp with an extra squirt of fish sauce. No crushed peanuts.

Aunty Sue and my father both ate theirs with spoonfuls of dry chilies scooped over their noodles. One look and you'd know that their dish was more dangerous than tasty. It was an unspoken contest between them, who could take the heat.

Aunty Sue won. She always did. She ate without water, while my father consumed glass after glass. Sweat beaded his temples. His nose ran.

"Very good," my father said.

"Thank you for cooking," said my mother.

"We're not done yet," I said. I jumped off my chair and got dessert. It looked like a ship disaster in a white sea, stiffened arms and legs poking out from the surface. "I made something sweet."

My father rose from the table and brought his plate to the sink. "*Eem,*" he said. I'm full. "Next time." He went downstairs and continued putting.

"Crazy," said my mother. "Making such a mess."

Before I could hang my head low, Aunty Sue took out R2D2 and began sucking on his android head. She made satisfied *mmmmmm* sounds. "Excellent," she said. "Taste very delicious."

In 1965, while Aunty Sue was in Chulalongkorn University's nursing program in Bangkok, her supervisor presented her with an irresistible opportunity. He had received a letter from the Hospital of Englewood in Chicago, asking whether there were nurses willing to come across the ocean and start new jobs, new lives. Englewood, located in a rough neighborhood, needed nurses. They'd provide housing, and the pay was double what she was earning in Thailand.

Aunty Sue did not take long to answer. Already, she dreamt of cruising American streets in an American muscle car, a Thunderbird, even though she didn't know how to drive. She dreamt of the food: hamburgers, pizzas, cookies and cakes. She dreamt of non-squatting toilets and air-conditioning. Yes, she would go. No doubt about it.

Back then, Aunty Sue was involved with an alcoholic, a man who hit her after he finished a bottle of Johnnie Walker. Once he hit her when he was sober, and she knew he had more than a problem with alcohol. This man was the only love interest my aunt had ever mentioned. She never spoke of another, and I assumed there were none. But he had left a deep scar, deep enough to carry her across the world, putting uncountable miles between her and her family. Perhaps he was the reason Aunty Sue never dated again, never sought the companionship of the opposite sex; I became the only man in her life.

By nature, my aunt is a social creature, one who always sought the companionship of others. She set people at ease immediately, always asking inquisitive questions, and soon enough, people would begin to tell her their life stories, their secrets, would admit their deepest insecurities. I have seen this happen on countless occasions. Once, my mother's childhood friend visited from Florida—a woman my aunt had never met—and within half an hour, she disclosed the reason for her divorce, sobbing profusely onto my aunt's shoulder.

It was not surprising then, in the summer of 1968, that Aunty Sue would meet a timid Thai girl and begin a long-lasting friendship.

When she first arrived in Chicago, my aunt lived in the nurses' dormitory. Some windows in the dorm rooms were barred. Rumor had it the building used to be an asylum. My aunt, sensitive to the spirit world, often felt restless, as if there was someone sitting on her chest; the only way to breathe was to keep moving.

Each floor had a small kitchen unit. Aunty Sue spent most of her off-time watching everyone cook. The black nurses explained to her that the secret to collard greens was the salted ham hock; the Korean nurses said the longer the beef marinated, the better the *bugogi* would be; the Chinese told her, for stir-fries, the pan had to be so hot that when you spit in it, it would immediately evaporate. In Thailand, Aunty Sue's family hired house girls to do all the cooking, so she never received a proper education in the kitchen. Until Englewood, she didn't even know how to boil an egg.

After a month in the country, Aunty Sue became curious about the quiet nurse down the hall. "Never come out of room," she said. "Your mama like mouse, quick to hiding."

One evening, she knocked on my mother's door. Her knock was met by a startled brown eye. My aunt put her hands together and bowed her head. The door opened wider, and my mother stood in rose-colored pajamas that floated above the knee, pink curlers in her hair. The tops of her cheeks were dotted with freckles. Shyly, my mother returned Aunty Sue's gesture. The smell of burnt garlic emanated from my mother's room. Aunty Sue wrinkled her nose. She didn't, however, criticize. Instead, she asked what smelled so delicious. My mother shrugged. Radishes and eggs, she said. My aunt told her it was one of her favorite dishes, and she hoped one day she could eat some with her. Backing into her room, my mother said she worked the morning shift, so she'd better get to bed.

Two days later, Aunty Sue came back. She asked whether my mother had eaten yet, a traditional Thai greeting. My mother told her radishes and eggs. The next day my aunt knocked again and asked the same question. Radishes and eggs, my mother said.

One night, Aunty Sue decided to cook her first meal—fried rice. She crept into the kitchen at midnight when the floor was quiet. She minced three cloves of garlic, the paring knife flimsy in her hand. She finely chopped two stalks of green onion and sliced chicken breasts into little bite-sized pieces. The secret, she remembered one of her friends saying, was to use day-old rice. If you fried freshly made rice, the dish would come out mushy.

In a hot pan, she poured a dollop of peanut oil and tossed in the garlic. Then she added two eggs and the chicken. She waited until the chicken browned and the eggs scrambled dry before scooping the rice into the pan, breaking the hard pellets down with a spatula. Then she mixed in a few shakes of white soy sauce and a pinch of sugar. Last, she sprinkled the scallions over the rice.

Proud of her first dish, Aunty Sue wanted to share it with someone. She walked past each room, spatula and frying pan in hand. She pressed her ear against the wooden doors and listened, hoping someone was still awake. When she came to my mother's door, she heard crying. Timidly, she knocked. My mother opened it, eyes red and wet.

"Right away, I think too much radish and egg. Not good to eat every day. I telling your mama it happen to me all the time." My mother laughed, wiping the streaks from her cheeks. Aunty Sue offered her the fried rice and my mother nodded and stepped aside. In the corner of her room were an electric burner and a blackened frying pan, and along the window ledge were jars of radishes and eggs.

They sat on the bed, the frying pan between them, spooning mouthfuls of fried rice. My mother admitted to her tears. She missed Thailand, missed her family, missed her father most of all. My aunt knew how she felt. She wrote letters to her family every day. She tried to distract herself by meeting people and going out into the city. If she didn't, she'd be cooped up in her room crying, too. My mother said she was scared. My aunt said, don't be. She had a friend.

They talked until the sun came up and the rice disappeared from the pan, leaving swirls of glistening oil. Before Aunty Sue left, she asked whether the rice was too salty. My mother shook her head. She said it was the best thing she had eaten since she arrived in America.

It had been a bad month. Some months were better than others. High school boys ding-dong-ditched our house past midnight until my father walked out with a gun—a toy that glinted in the front door light; our mailbox was found off its base five consecutive days, so concaved it looked flat; the five-year-old boy who lived behind our house called Aunty Sue a son-of-a-bitch and sprinkled water from a hose on her; and on an evening in early spring, the evening that made Aunty Sue enroll me in martial arts the next day, I disgraced my family.

Aunty Sue and I had gone grocery shopping without my mother, who had decided to stay home and read. As my aunt pulled the Chevy station wagon into the driveway, I noticed three boys riding bikes at the other end of McVicker. I recognized a couple of them, older brothers of Jason and Robby in my fifth-grade class. One of them cruised without any hands on the handlebars, his arms dangling at his sides. The other had hair the color of pumpkin, and the last one wore a White Sox cap backward.

I heard their laughter, loud and conspiratorial. The closer they came the farther I wanted to be, unseen and away from Aunty Sue.

"I have to go to the bathroom," I said quickly, sprinting toward the house. My aunt asked if I could at least take one grocery bag in, but I was already through the front door.

I headed for the bay window, parting the sheer curtain a sliver to look out without being caught. I knew what would happen. I had developed a sixth sense for trouble.

Aunty Sue unloaded the car, taking a brown grocery bag out and placing it on the driveway. A roll of paper towels tumbled from the bag and into the street right as the boys passed.

They circled back.

The one with his hands to his side pulled the corners of his eyes. The pumpkin-haired one rode over the roll. The third one chanted: "Chinky, chinky, chink-eee." He sounded like a bell.

Aunty Sue eyed them unflinchingly.

Before they left, one of them spit a high arcing loogy that splattered at my aunt's feet. They zoomed down the block toward 95th, their laughter fading in the distance.

Aunty Sue turned away, her body rigid for long seconds before she hoisted up two bags in her small arms and walked toward the house. Usually, she was the calm one in our family, the woman who talked my mother out of her anger and distrust for the world, the one who restored order. That evening, however, I had never seen Aunty Sue angrier.

As she made it up the driveway, I burned with humiliation. Would Bruce Lee run away? Hell no. Bruce would have kicked ass, shirtless and pulsating with muscles like in the last scene of *Enter the Dragon.* He'd push the boys off their bikes, their legs scraping against the coarse blacktop. When they were down, he'd walk on their heads like on stepping stones in a river.

I wasn't Bruce.

I was scared of those boys. I was even more scared of something my eleven-year-old mind could not comprehend then. I was scared of my Thai-ness. I turned my back on Aunty Sue because I was embarrassed of her in the same way I began to be embarrassed of my family. I looked like them, talked like them, and ate like them. It was the "them" in my blood that set me apart while all I wanted was to be part of something. I began to see my family in the way the neighborhood saw us, the way my classmates saw me. We stood out. My mother placed a shot glass of coffee on the top step leading into the back door for the invisible spiritual guardian of our home. My father clinked and rattled when he walked with all his Buddha pendants hanging outside his shirt, something I had wanted to emulate when I was six, but now was discomfited by. Aunty Sue fried salted fish out in the garage so the entire block smelled like a fish aisle gone bad.

I didn't want to be "them" anymore. I wanted to be normal.

I went out the door to help my aunt. I opened my arms and waited for a bag of groceries, smiling as big as I could, pretending not to know what had happened, not to notice her darkened face. She brushed past me.

"You left me alone," Aunty Sue said in Thai. "*Pen puchai rue?*" Are you a man?

My father worked the evening shift at Kentile factory a block or two off Pulaski Avenue. He often bragged about how Kentile was owned by the Kennedy family, and how, once, an actual Kennedy came to do an inspection. Which Kennedy it was my father didn't know, but he was sure it wasn't the one that got shot.

A chemist, he researched ways to make a more durable bathroom and kitchen floor. He was efficient at what he did. Within months of being hired at Kentile, he received a supervisor position, a daunting honor for my father. Then, he could barely speak English, let alone oversee a bunch of men who thought he was short. My father persevered and gained the respect of his workers. He learned commands and curses in three different languages: *Jeste głupi* (Polish, "You are stupid."); *Mierda* (Spanish, "Shit."); *Goddamn, muterfackar* (English, self-explanatory).

If I tagged along to the hardware store, my father made it a point to show me the tile section, waving his hands along the rows and rows of flooring. "Touch this," he said. I ran my fingers over the bumps on the ceramic. "And this." This one was smooth, my finger gliding in figure eights. "I make them. All of them. I make color. Make thick or thin. I mix the chemical." It was the chemicals that burned my father's skin, leaving his hands spotted and red raw. When I was four, I took pride in rubbing lotion on his hands, rough and callused, as he watched TV. I wanted hands like my father, the bubble of hardness on the stem of his middle fingers, the thick, branch-ing veins. Mine were plump and soft. Mine had no veins, no hard spots. Mine looked lifeless, like the mannequins' at de-partment stores. When my father patted my head, I felt the strength in his fingers. He told me these were the hands of a man who lived a hard life. He'd rather my hands be soft forev-er, like a cloud. My father sculpted a cloud with his hands and then blew it into the air, where, in my imagination, it floated wherever I went.

Because of his work schedule, I rarely saw my father except on weekends. His absence made me yearn for him more. His absence meant Aunty Sue took on paternal duties.

It was my aunt's hand that guided me on the bicycle. I tested out the new moves I learned at Sang's, the Tae Kwon Do Dojo she enrolled me in on Archer Avenue. She was my Jim Mc-Mahon, Chicago Bears quarterback, without the spiked hair, chucking a Nerf football over our two-story house, the sweet-est spiral I'd ever seen. She put up a basketball hoop in the backyard, and laid down green outdoor carpeting so the tiny court resembled Boston Garden.

At the same time, because I grew up in a house with essen-tially two mothers, I received a different education from most boys. Each night, I helped my mother put pink rollers in her hair, and every three months, I pasted Revlon hair coloring onto my mother's and aunt's heads.

My mother taught me the artistry of a seamstress—to stitch up tears in my clothes, sew on missing buttons, and work her Singer sewing machine. I helped my mother pick out designs for her Thai dresses.

And I gardened. In the early spring months, when the ground had thawed, I dug the earth where Aunty Sue's tomatoes, zuc-chinis, Thai peppers, and bitter melons would grow. She'd grab a clump of soil, sniff it, and then let it sift through her fingers. This, she said, will be a good growing year. Every year was a good growing year.

I began to wonder what it meant to be a man. Was it unusual for a nine-year-old boy to dress up in his mother's clothing, put on a wig, and dance around like a teen pop idol, making his mother and aunt roll with laughter? I had no basis for comparison. I saw my father on weekends, and was so delighted to have him near that I never took note of what was "man" about him.

Mike and Kevin weren't men. They were weird boys.

In conversations about their fathers, they developed a bravado of masculinity. Father conversations only existed on Fridays when we made the long trek—one whole mile—to a comic book store. There, we spent our allowances on *X-Men, Spiderman, The Punisher,* and occasionally *The Fantastic Four.* The three of us had gotten into comic books for different reasons: I marveled at the artwork and potential value, Mike relished the storylines, and Kevin only bought comics because Mike and I did.

This time we compared Batman—whom we despised—to our fathers.

"I saw my dad bench four hundred pounds," Kevin said. "I'm sure Batman can't bench three hundred. That's like six of me." Kevin flexed his small arms that looked like thin pipes.

"That's only three of Ira," Mike said and laughed.

"Shut up," I said.

Mike patted me on the back, a gesture that said he didn't mean it. We cut through someone's yard, ducking under the limbs of a pine tree, and then traveled the long sidewalks of Moody Avenue.

"Batman's a wimp anyway," said Mike. "My dad would totally beat him down even if Batdork wore his stupid utility belt. The other day my dad came home with a broken nose. He got into a fight with someone in his hockey league. I swear his nose looked like this." He pushed his nose to the extreme right. "It was the coolest thing I ever saw in my life." He sounded nasal.

It was my turn. I was sure my father couldn't bench three hundred pounds. I couldn't picture him on ice skates, wearing an oversized hockey mask. My father was short and walked like a penguin. He listened to FM 100, the elevator music station. He wore large square glasses that tinted in the sun and lightened indoors. The only sport he played was golf. If he were a comic book hero, he'd be the Thai Putter, the letters TP on his chest.

"My dad," I said, "fought a gorilla and won. Batman has never fought a gorilla."

"No way," Kevin said in awe.

"When?" Mike said. "Where?"

Mike and Kevin were on either side of me, hovering close to my face, ready for another story about my father. I never wanted to be left out of our conversations, so I made up tall tales, exaggerated the strength and powers of my father. Mike and Kevin believed everything I said as long as I gave them a story. A story was what I was good at.

That year my father had just gotten cable TV, and I remember watching *Circle of Iron,* a 1978 movie cowritten by Bruce Lee. In the beginning, the main character faced off against a monkey-like creature and defeated it; it was one of many fights in the movie. As the character moved forward in his journey, he faced more odd fighters. The movie was meant to teach Eastern philosophies to a mainstream Western audience; it had multiple layers of complexity, but all I remember was it kicked a lot of ass.

I told Mike and Kevin that my father fought a gorilla in one of the stages before he became a master of *Muay Thai,* Thai boxing. I provided an exotic setting, under a canopy of coconut trees. I described the gorilla spectators hitting their chests, their way of clapping. I went into great detail about the monkey's attack and how my father parried it. The battle was long, but my father was eventually victorious.

At the end of my story, I said, "It's a Thai thing." There was never any dispute about anything that was a Thai thing. Thailand was so alien to them that I could've said, "In Thailand men have the babies," and they would have fallen for it.

"Your dad must be really tough," Kevin said.

"X-Men tough," said Mike.

"Yep," I said proudly.

When we reached the comic book store, the owner handed us bags of our favorite comics. It was a quick exchange. We were regulars. We didn't dilly-dally.

On our way back, we walked quickly, anxious to get home and read our purchases. We sometimes played tag down the block or raced each other from stop sign to stop sign. That day, we took to insults. Dork nose. Idiot head. Dookie face. Our laughter bounced off the trees, the parked cars along the street, the aluminum siding of the houses we passed. Even though our voices rang loud, we felt like we were the only people in the world, the three us—Butthead, Poop Nose, and Pee Pee Wipe.

Then Mike called Kevin a fairy.

The image of Tinkerbell from Peter Pan flashed in my head, a tiny dancing light. Kevin didn't look like Tinkerbell. If he did, he was a skinny, stringy-haired Tinkerbell, a super-ugly Tinkerbell.

Kevin stopped. "I'm not a fairy."

"You walk like one," Mike said. He imitated Kevin, prancing on the tips of his toes, as if he wore heels. He stuck out his chest and chin. Then he laughed, but no one laughed with him so he stopped.

"I don't," said Kevin. He plunged his hands into his pockets.

"He doesn't," I said. "Fairies fly. They don't walk."

"Not that kind of fairy." Mike carelessly twirled his bag of comics around his fingers, and I winced, imagining bent pages and broken spines. "Fairies are guys who like guys."

"I like you," I said. "I must be a fairy."

"No, stupid. Like in the love sense. In the you-want-to-kiss-me-on-the-lips sense. There are three ways you can tell someone's a fairy. One, by his voice. Fairies talk like someone's holding their tongues, like weird snakes. Two, they like girl singers like Debbie Gibson, or Tiffany, or Belinda Carlisle. Three, they walk like girls."

"I'm not a fairy, Mike," Kevin said. He stalked on ahead.

Mike ran to catch up to Kevin. He could never let one of us be mad at him for long. We three had only each other. This couldn't change.

I hung back and thought about Mike's list of what constituted a fairy.

At Harnew, I was still working on pronouncing my "s" sound correctly. Though my accent had lessened considerably, I sometimes slurred. I had a lisp, especially when I became excited; words would flood my mouth, gushing forth uncontrollably.

And the singers I liked to listen to *were* Debbie, Tiffany, and Belinda. I sang their songs in the shower. In my imagination, I stood in front of a crowd of thousands in the Rosemont Horizon Auditorium, belting out Tiffany's I "Think We're Alone Now" in perfect pitch. The crowd screamed for an encore and I gave them Debbie Gibson's "Only in My Dreams."

And my walk. I didn't know what to think of my walk. I never looked at myself in that way. But now, it was all I could think of. Every step home, I questioned whether I fluttered like a fairy. I watched my feet. Made sure my back had a slight slouch to it.

Mike and Kevin had made amends, but they were quiet. The word *fairy,* unlike ca-ca nose or fart face, had shifted the balance of the day; we were all under a spell.

I began taking note of how other men walked. Some, especially the police officers in *Hill Street Blues,* a drama on NBC about a police precinct in Chicago, walked stiffly, their upper bodies tight; every step they took seemed important and serious and a bit robotic. Mr. T from the *A-Team* walked with his arms out to the sides because of his bulging muscles. He sneered as he took his steps. In *Welcome Back, Kotter* reruns, the Sweathogs all had distinct walks, their bodies limp like noodles. They swaggered, their arms moving to a mysterious beat in their heads.

That was the walk I worked on—my own cool, suave swagger.

Aunty Sue noticed my different walk. She was cooking up some spring rolls in the garage while I played football by myself, using targets—the light post, the garbage can, the car—as my receivers. After every down, I sported my new walk.

"Is leg hurting?" Aunty Sue asked.

"Nope." I took one step and swaggered, took another and swaggered. My hand moved like a giant wave.

"Why walk like that then?" she said.

"Like what?"

"Like that." My aunt imitated my walk. She had silver tongs in her hand and a shower cap on her head to keep her hair out of the food. As she mocked my walk, she looked like a wounded soldier dragging her dead leg, a metal claw for a hand.

"I don't look like that." I lessened my swagger.

"Walk like handicap people. Like crazy man."

Embarrassed, I swaggered quickly into the house.

Finding my man's walk wasn't the only thing I practiced. One day, my next-door neighbor Jack, a World War II vet, adjusted himself. I sat on the front doorstep, reading *Black Belt,* a martial arts magazine, and right there, as Jack was gathering apples from his tree, he grabbed his crotch and moved it. He didn't know I was watching. A few minutes later, he did it again.

Jack Hunt was the toughest man I had ever met, despite being in his sixties. He came over to fix anything mechanical while my father was at work, our personal handyman. I rode on the back of his riding mower as we zoomed back and forth across his yard. He told violent war stories about the Japanese and their tricky combat tactics, sometimes acting out his self-defense moves to illustrate the severity of the situation. But there was the gentle side of Jack. The times when he dropped bags of zucchini and rhubarb at our door step. (My aunt never made sense out of rhubarb.) Times he would get teary when talking about his daughters and niece and nephew in Florida. He and his wife, Helen, took care of my mother and aunt, and became their lifelong friends, the only true white friends they ever had.

But that day, unbeknownst to Jack, he was introducing me to this other world I never knew existed. A world of adjusters. I began to note that other men did it. Even super-athletes like Carlton Fisk, who after an unbelievable out throw to second went down there and shifted. Michael Jordan adjusted after dunking on Patrick Ewing, who adjusted a few minutes later. The men I saw on a daily basis adjusted: my school principal, Mr. Malkovich, who would do a little dip and move his hands quickly across the area; my father, even he adjusted, a secret and swift move that could be misconstrued as a regular hand motion. This was what men did. Men adjusted. It was a club, a brotherhood.

My mother caught me adjusting while I was practicing my sidekicks on a couple of pillows I balanced on top of the couch.

"Why do that?" my mother said, coming in from the back-yard with a laundry basket cradled in her arms.

"Do what?"

"Scratching? Need to go to hospital?"

"No."

"Let me see."

"No."

"I nurse."

"Mom," I whined.

"Why scratching?"

"I wasn't scratching." I put a pillow back on top of the couch. "I was moving."

My mother dropped the basket and started laughing, her hand over her mouth. "Too young to move anything. Nothing to move."

She was right.

This journey toward manhood was frustrating. I was still a boy after all, and would remain one for another few years. But boys never want to be boys; they are forever practicing to be men, and for me, to be a man meant I was not a disgrace to my family, meant I was ready for anything, even bike-riding bullies.

Mike and I were walking home from school. The sun shone across Harnew's playground, casting long, late afternoon shadows.

I punched at his shadow, and he punched at mine. Then we concentrated on walking, making sure not to step on any cracks on the sidewalk. Though we knew it was impossible, we somewhat believed in the children's rhyme: *Step on a crack and you'll break your mother's back.*

Mike told me he finished King's *Salem's Lot,* and decided that when he grew up he wanted to become a vampire.

"You're too short," I said.

"Vampires can be short," he said. "I've never heard of a fat, Thai vampire."

"Shut up," I said.

As we passed the faculty parking lot, two high schoolers cut through the back of someone's yard and followed us. I felt uneasy immediately. I wanted to get to Mike's as fast as possible so we could pop in the movie *Clue* and watch it for the twentieth time. But something stopped me. Perhaps it was my Tae Kwon Do lessons that made me feel more confident about myself. Perhaps I wanted to make up for what I hadn't done months ago when I shamed my aunt. Regardless, that afternoon, I spun around and fronted the high schoolers and said, "Why don't you shut the heck up?"

Mike's eyes widened.

My hands were on my hips. Everything seemed beyond my control.

The high schoolers were twins, or at least brothers who were nearly identical. Both had brown hair swept to the right. Both wore leather bomber jackets with flannel shirts poking out of the bottom, one red, the other green.

Red said, "What?"

I stared at him. "I heard you talking about us, so shut up."

"We didn't say anything," Green said.

"But what if we did?" said Red.

Mike looked fearfully from me to the twins. Then he got brave, too. He stuck out his chest and said, "My friend's a black belt. He'll kick your butt."

I wasn't a black belt. Not for another six months.

The twins laughed, bodies bumping against each other. Green got into a fighting stance. "OK, Black Belt, show me."

I immediately put my fists up.

"I'd like to see this," said Red, clapping his hands.

"Kick him in the head," Mike said.

"Yeah, kick me in the head."

Green playfully swiped at me a few times.

"I don't want to hurt you," I said.

"Just show us," Red said. He stood behind his brother, Mike behind me.

"Come on, Black Belt." Green made mock karate sounds like the ones on badly dubbed kung fu movies.

"This is too much," said Red, his hand on his stomach, laughing.

"Nail him, Ira," Mike whispered. "Nail him good."

I meant to stop the kick short. Stop it in mid-air before it hit his temple. I would hold the pose. Show off my balance. Win a fight without fighting.

I swung my right leg and connected hard.

Red stopped laughing. Green put his hand to the side of his head. Mike said, "Holy shit!"

After the initial shock, Green charged. I stepped back, ready to strike again, but his brother jumped between us.

"You're dead," said Green.

"No, he isn't," said his brother. "He's, like, ten."

"He kicked me in the head." A line of blood streaked along the side of his cheek.

"Yes, yes, he did," Mike said, grinning.

Green went for Mike. His brother pushed him away again.

"You need to chill," said Red. "He's a sixth grader."

"Fifth," said Mike, putting five fingers up.

"We are sophomores," the twin said. "Soph-mores."

"Fine. Whatever." Green picked up his books and crossed the street, mumbling.

Red shrugged. "Nice kick," he said. He jogged to catch up with his brother.

When we arrived at his place, Mike couldn't stop talking about the kick. He got on the phone and called Kevin. I overheard Kevin's awestruck "No ways." Mike tried to reenact the kick, but he couldn't get his foot past my chest. He wanted me to teach him how to kick like that. We spent the rest of the afternoon roundhousing dirty laundry.

The next day, Mike told everyone at Harnew Elementary. *Ira beat up a high schooler. Ira beat up a high schooler.* No more name-calling because Ira would kill you. If you take Ira's Doritos he may karate chop your fingers off.

"Let's open a karate school," Mike said.

We were shooting free throws in the playground. It had rained the night before, so the unleveled parts of the blacktop brimmed with dirty water.

Kevin passed the ball to me. I shot and made it.

"You're a black belt," Mike said, leaning on the basketball pole. The ball bounced to him, and he fumbled with it before stilling it in his hands. He bounce-passed to me.

"I'm not a black belt." I shot. Two for two.

"They don't know that," Kevin said.

"Kev's right," Mike said. "We'll make signs. 'Learn the ancient art of karate from the third grader who took down a high schooler.' We could do it at my house, in the backyard. Five dollars a lesson. Do you know how many comics we can get for five dollars?"

I contemplated their idea. Five extra dollars worth of comics? "I'm in," I said. *Swish.*

> Want to learn Karate?
> Come and train with a master.
> Five dollars.
> Friday at four.
> Mike's house.
> Be there.

We waited. Mike, Kevin and I sat on a swing set in Mike's backyard. Mike's swing was so rusted you could get tetanus by looking at it.

"No one's coming," Kevin said. He was always a pessimist. A pessimist in yellow sweats.

"Chill out," Mike said.

I sat on the swing in my uniform, pretending to look like a master—stern and deep in thought. I had ordered a black belt through one of my martial arts magazines. It was pure black, the blackest thing I'd ever seen. Blacker than my father's hair. It was so black I was afraid people would assume it was a fake.

Someone knocked on the outside of Mike's brown metal fence. The fence vibrated. Kevin looked at me, smiling. He mouthed five dollars. Mike darted to the fence door and opened it. Dave—aka Turtle—walked in, his hands deep in his pockets. We called him Turtle because he liked turtles and brought some to Show and Tell in first grade. Mike talked to Dave, things I couldn't hear. Dave took one of his hands out his pockets and gave Mike a few dollars and a lot of change. After Dave came the Soderstrom brothers. Then Tracy Gilligan, who I secretly liked. I tugged at my fake belt. She waved at me from a distance while handing Mike change. Then Mark Parsons rode in on his bike; he was a star soccer player. Then Matt Menneghini, the fastest and coolest kid in school; all the girls had crushes on him, but he appeared not to care. Then Beth Everett, the gymnast who could do a backbend with ease. Then Dave Siddle, who could moonwalk like he was on a sheet of ice. Then the Josh-es. Then Tanya. Then Rich and Mitch and Mark.

Mike's backyard was filled with kids and bikes and Mike was smiling, fistful of dollars in his hand, change bulging in his pockets, and Kevin was smiling and talking to Turtle, and I wanted to smile but couldn't because I was a master and masters didn't smile.

Before we got started I demonstrated how hard my shins were. I stole twenty of my aunt's bamboo sticks she used in her garden to stake tomatoes. They were as thin as a pencil, but hard. With one swift kick, I broke through all of them. Tracy clapped. Then I brought Kevin out and kicked over his head. Then I told Mike to grab my uniform, and I swiftly brought him to the ground with a wristlock.

They listened. They watched. I taught them various blocks—high block, low block—and a few kicks—roundhouse, jumping front kick. I told Tracy to punch me and complimented her ability to bruise.

When everyone left, Tracy stayed behind. I couldn't look at her. I pretended to be deep in thought like a Shaolin monk, observing the delicate budding leaves of the oak tree and how the light from the setting sun pierced through the spaces in the branches. "Ira," she said, "did you really beat up a high schooler?"

"I kicked him in the head," I said.

She smiled. "That's so cool."

"Yeah." I began to rock on my heels.

She rocked on hers.

I noticed our breathing was in sync.

"Well," she said, "I guess I'll see you at school?"

"Yeah. Right. School."

Tracy turned to leave, and I willed my eyes to follow her pretty purple sweats as she made it through the opening in Mike's fence. She turned one last time and waved with her fingers.

Kevin and Mike puckered their lips together and made kissy noises, and I turned away, embarrassed and exhilarated.

Tracy Gilligan moved away the next school year, but not without kicking Andrea—a bully—in the shins, which I was proud to have witnessed, and not without bumping my hand once on a walk home. I want to say that Tracy and I kissed by the maple tree in Harnew's baseball fields, that we read poetry and planned our futures together. I want to say that Tracy was my first true love. But the truth was I liked Tracy, but not as much as I liked my Nerf football. And she probably liked me, but not more than her Cabbage Patch Doll. That's how it was for eleven-year-olds.

My father and aunt kept a quiet distance. They talked as if they were friendly strangers. On weekend mornings, when my mother hung laundry outside, my father would wake up to my aunt in the kitchen and me watching my cartoons downstairs. There would be a prolonged silence before he'd say good morning, *sawasdee,* too formally. My aunt would fold her hands together and bow her head. Then he would hover around in the kitchen like a confused guest, opening and closing the refrigerator, sighing heavily, until my aunt suggested he sit down, she'd made rice porridge. Thank you, he said. You're welcome, she said and placed a steaming bowl in front of him. Thank you, he said again. You're welcome, she said. He ate. She kept busy.

I sometimes watched them from downstairs, my attention diverted from *Pee-wee's Playhouse.* I sometimes forced them to talk.

"Tell *Pau* about how I kicked the soccer ball over the fence," I told my aunt.

"Yes, very strong," she said.

"*Dee mark,*" said my father. Excellent.

"Tell *Pau* about the new bead I got in Boy Scouts."

"Shiny," she said.

"Excellent," he said.

What was it that kept them apart? When my mother was with them, they spoke freely, but alone, they kept to themselves. I don't think my father minded Aunty Sue usurping his paternal duties; I never sensed he was jealous over me. In fact,

I believed he was thankful that it wasn't his arms and legs that were always bruised, that it wasn't his rib I cracked while playing football.

In many ways, I believe he saw Aunty Sue as a traditional Thai servant, one who swept the porch, made the beds, took care of the young, and bought dinner at the market. Indeed, Aunty Sue did all these things. She made our house spotless, gathering my Transformers and G.I. Joe action figures scattered across the plush carpet. She helped my mother with the bills, and made sure the cars were taken in for their yearly emissions test. She was the first to brave a snowy morning, pushing the shovel along our lengthy driveway. She sated our hunger with succulent Thai meals. My father never thanked Aunty Sue for all the things she did around the house. These everyday chores never needed recognition.

Ironically, the house we lived in on McVicker Avenue, Aunty Sue owned. It had been her gift to my mother after hearing the news of her pregnancy. She had placed a down payment on the house, and the plan was my father would help with the monthly installments. He never did, my mother always having to make up for his half.

Still, despite my father's faults, Aunty Sue yielded to him. She instructed me to always obey my father and my mother, above all things.

"Even Buddha?" I said once.

"Yes," she said, "above Buddha."

We needed a new battery for the sump pump, which had died the night before after a persistent rain that lasted for most of the day. Water had seeped into the basement. My father was more upset than usual. He kept asking my aunt why she hadn't gotten a new battery the day before. Aunty Sue apologized over and over, pulling bills out of her own wallet for the battery. My father grabbed the money and shoved the bills into his pocket. His anger came out in a series of exasperated sighs and sulky whines. In his deep exhales he was saying, *why do you waste my weekend with this work, why must I clean up after your incompetence, why do we keep you?*

My father left and I tagged along, wanting to tap into his knowledge of manhood. He was not in the mood for a barrage of questions.

On the way to the hardware store: "If someone calls me a name, can I kick him?"

In the parking lot: "When does hair start growing on my chest?"

While passing lumber: "Do men make their voices deep?"

In batteries: "Our teacher said one of the greatest men in history was George Washington. He chopped down a cherry tree. Jack has a cherry tree."

In checkout: "So do you fight?"

Back in the car: "When will I be a man?"

With the other questions, my father simply ignored me or grunted. After this last one, however, he slammed his palm on the car horn and kept it there for a few seconds. We hadn't pulled out of the parking lot. He stared straight ahead. I shut up. Then my father turned to me.

"You ten—"

"Eleven," I corrected.

"Eleven," my father said. "Not man."

"I want to be one." I talked to the gearshift. I traced my finger along the seams of the car seat. "I want to be like you."

My father drew in a deep breath and let it out slowly. I felt his hand on the back of my neck. I tilted my face to see him smiling and shaking his head.

"Must wait," he said.

"A long time?"

He shrugged. "Not very." He gave my neck a tiny squeeze. "Very hard to be man. Confusing. Not always good." His voice seemed far. He sank into his seat. "One thing," he looked at me. "*Puji mai wing nee,*" he said. A man never runs away.

My father gave my neck another squeeze and leaned in to start the car. I sat and wondered if he knew what I had done to Aunty Sue that evening after our trip to the grocery store. To my knowledge she never told anyone, not even my mother. But as I sat there in my father's car, elevator music in the background, it was the only thing I could think of, the only thing that made sense. I didn't know for another eight years what he really meant. I didn't know that he was speaking more about himself in that moment than he had shared with me in his entire life. My father was an enigma. I told stories to Mike and Kevin, to myself, creating a myth of a man, a comic book hero. And I believed my stories about my father, that he possessed in him infinite knowledge of the world. That he *was* beyond Buddha. And his words, his lesson, I took to heart, repeating it over and over. *A man never runs away. A man never runs away. A man never runs . . .*

My Father's Swing

When I was born, my father ordered an old Japanese table from a vendor in Thailand. This would be the table that held all my accomplishments. It stood a foot off the floor. The black top was inlaid with mother-of-pearl in a design of a peacock spreading its colorful feathers around a pole tree. For years, a lone trophy sat in the middle of the table. I remember running my hands over the little gold golfer and petting its arms and legs. It was polished to a gleam. When the sun came through our front window, the head of the gold golfer reflected a brilliant shine. It was the shine that attracted me, the shimmering gold. It was my father's trophy, one in his entire life.

My father used to tell me the story of his only victory, and it resonated in my memory like all of his stories—fantastic and unreal. I believed everything: the largest tree in the world that blocked his view of the 18th green, the ninety-foot putt he sank to win the tournament. He compared the spectators cheering him to the noisy fans at Soldier Field during a Bears football game. He said rose petals floated down from the sky and his golf clubs began to glow. I listened in awe to my father's roller coaster voice—slow and soft before plummeting in a rush of breathless adrenaline.

What I knew of him I knew from his stories. I had spent most of my life trying to figure out who he was, putting his past together like a puzzle, hoping I had every piece.

My father was born in 1934 in Ayuthaya, the old capital of the Kingdom of Siam. Ayuthaya is a city of ruin, a place of charred and crumbled temples and decapitated Buddhas, of battles and wars against the Burmese in the late 1700s. My father said he sometimes heard strange battle cries, the thundering feet of an army of elephants, and the ghostly clanging of swords. Years later, when I visited Ayuthaya, I couldn't shake the feeling of sadness that lingered around every corner. It was here my father's life began.

I liked to imagine my father was born in the midst of some cataclysmic storm, a monsoon that brought about torrents of rain and devastating winds, and when the clouds lifted and the sun broke through the sky, rising from the debris was this boy, alive and unharmed. This was how heroes were born, like the Kents finding baby Superman in a tiny rocket sent from the planet Krypton before it exploded.

The truth was I knew nothing of my father's birth. I gathered he lived a Tom Sawyer boyhood—adventurous, filled with danger and mischief. When he was old enough to take care of himself—eleven or twelve—he took to the outdoors, sleeping outside and eating the fish he caught. Once, when I was six, he put me on his knee and I leaned on his chest, amazed at his tales. "I kill snake and eat it. Snake this big." He stretched out his arms as wide as they could go. "Bigger than this. One time I jump into river to get fish and fish bite my ankle." He pulled up his left pant leg and pointed to a small round scar on his calf. "They call fish piranha here." He told me about the crazy dog that had taken a chunk out of his arm. More stories. More scars. His body was endless with wounds. I touched them, feeling the indentations in his skin, marks that never completely healed.

The reasons why my father decided to come to America remain fuzzy. He was a dreamer. He often thought up improbable ideas: opening a restaurant or spa, owning a gas station, getting into the canned food business. America must've seemed the ideal place for his dreams, a land in which he thought his life would begin. The problem was my father already had a life. He was married and had a daughter named *Noo,* mouse, whom I met once; we both regarded each other with genuine curiosity. Still, like many immigrants, for him America was about possibility, the pull of which was too much for my father to ignore. He was a man who believed in signs, whose hobby was fortune telling. He must've seen it in the astrological grids he drew and kept in his back pocket. He must've asked the stars and they told him this was to be his destiny.

My mother had a different story: My father ran away. He ran away from his first wife and daughter. He ran away from the Thailand heat to the harsh Chicago winters on an illegal student visa. He ran away from the INS when they invaded the steel factories where he worked. In the midst of all this running, my father managed to get married and have a son, work at a legitimate job as a chemist, and most important, play golf nearly every weekend.

When I was three, my father took me to the driving range under the Cicero overpass, neighboring a truck yard. I dragged along one plastic club. He told me to sit still on a paint-chipped bench while he hit golf balls toward the empty cargo trailers in the distance. Each ball flew as high as the airplanes landing in Midway Airport down the street, zooming toward the two-hundred-fifty-yard marker. I had never seen anything fly so far. I was watching a magician.

After hitting a half-bucket of balls, my father motioned for me to hit one. I walked to the mat with my plastic club. I placed the ball on the rubber tee and tried to remember what my father's swing looked like. I even added a little grunt as I hit the ball, just like him. Even though the ball trickled three feet to the right, my father laughed and winked, and I, not knowing why he was laughing, laughed along with him.

My father started calling me *Mee Yai,* meaning "Big Bear," after his favorite golfer Jack Nicklaus, the "Golden Bear." For the next few years, every Saturday, we'd head for the driving range. My father bought two buckets of balls—one for me, the other for him. I usually went through mine quickly, no more than ten minutes. I put the ball on the tee and hit it without much thought. I loved the sound of the club making contact with the ball—a sharp, clean chop—loved watching the ball take flight and land and roll and roll and roll. "*Hen mai,* Dee?" I'd say. Did you see? My father would finish his swing and then clap his hands. "You will be pro," he'd say. "Big and strong like Jack. Maybe next time standing like this."

Through the years, the more I played, the more I measured myself against my father. I began to note flaws in his swing. He jerked the club back too quickly. His wrist broke harshly at the top, letting the club travel beyond parallel, almost touching his left shoulder. The swiftness of his hips over-torqued his body, spinning his front foot hard into the ground, the momentum pushing him off balance. Most of the time, he tumbled to his left side, unable to hold a controlled pose.

I never remarked on my father's swing, although I had dissected every facet of it. I began to realize, as most sons do at one point, that my father was flawed. Regardless of this revelation, he was still my teacher, my golfing coach. He knew more about the game, knew what I had done wrong, knew the ways to correct me. There were professionals with odd swings, like Lee Trevino, who aimed thirty yards to the left and cut the ball into the target, or Arnold Palmer, who whipped his arms around and over his head after impact, or Gary Player, who looked like linguine swinging at the ball. These were the golfing gods, men who took the game to another level, men my father wanted me to emulate and eventually become. He never sought to teach me his imperfect swing, or even theirs. He was allowing me to find my own.

Part of me, also, wanted to beat him. My father's score on eighteen holes hovered around 85–90, respectable for a weekend player. He drove the ball about two hundred yards. He possessed a wicked slice, was horrible from the sand trap, and was known to flub a few skittering rollers. Year after year, his game wasn't improving. Mine was. Each time I played the possibility of winning lingered in the back of my mind like an excited whisper. *Go get him.*

This desire to beat my father became my drive. I was more obsessed with golf than anything else in my life. It was all I thought about. When I wasn't at school, I was at home practicing my chips and putts. My mother once took a photo of me falling asleep on the couch, arms wrapped around my putter like a teddy bear. Various times throughout the day—waiting in line for the water fountain or in the outfield during softball games in gym—I found myself swinging an imaginary club, making minor corrections in hand position at impact.

My father took pride in my improvement. When we were at temple, he showed me off.

"He hits the ball as far as me now," my father said in Thai.

"Soon he will beat you," a doctor-friend said.

"Of course," said another. "He will beat everyone."

I felt awkward being the center of attention. In my mind, I knew I was good, but I had nothing to show for it except for my father's tales that began to grow and grow and grow, that made me into a wonder boy. The woman who sold *yentafo*— noodles in a red soup with squid, fish balls, and spinach—said I should donate money to the poor in Thailand when I became a famous golfer. The younger monks told me they would pray to Buddha to help me find the path to golfing glory. No one cared that I aced the math test last week. No one asked about my mother and Aunty Sue, who changed hospitals and shifts after Englewood closed down. Golfing wasn't just for me, wasn't just for my father, but for the Thai community waiting to cheer for someone of their own, waiting for a hero. The only worldly Thai celebrity then was Miss Universe 1965, Apasra Hongsakula, but only the older generation knew who she was.

My father talked about me so much I began to slip away and hide in some inconspicuous spot in temple. A week before my first tournament, I decided to sit on one of the many folding chairs in the main temple.

I had been jittery for the last two weeks. Whenever I thought about the tournament, I paced the house, my body restless with nervous energy. When I slept, I dreamt of humiliating defeats. In one of my dreams, I stepped onto the first hole and forgot how to play. I kept swinging the club and missing. The spectators booed.

Sitting in the empty temple, I begged Buddha to wake up and say something reassuring. I waited for his wisdom. I waited for a revelation.

A half hour later, my father found me and asked why I was sitting in the dark.

I shrugged, my fingers interlaced on my lap.

He sat beside me. "Ask for *boon* next week? Good luck?"

"Sorta," I said.

"Good," he said.

"I don't think you should talk about me anymore," I said. "It's a little weird."

He turned toward me, his arm draped on the back of the chair. "Before you born," he said, "I go see monk in Thailand. Most important monk. He say you born under same star as

Buddha." I stared at my father, wondering whether this was another story. The monk had told him I was a special baby, one who had the ability to change the world.

"This true," my father said. "Believe me?"

I wanted to.

"I dream about you, since I was boy. In past life, I always soldier. Always fighting, always dying. But you always born as leader, like prince. Born to—"

"Royalty," I said.

"*Chai.*" My father nodded. "Buddha, he send many dream about you. I see you every night, and every night you tell me not to be soldier anymore. You tell me to come here and you will follow. New life. New beginning. This true."

My father put his hands together and whispered a quick prayer. When he was done, he smiled. "When pro," he reached over to squeeze my neck, "everyone will talk. The country. The world."

In 1977, a core of Thai doctors and entrepreneurs formed the TGCC, the Thai Golf Club of Chicago. It was not a nationally recognized organization, but one open to Thais who loved the game of golf. The TGCC sponsored weekend tournaments from early spring through late fall. The Southern Illinois/Missouri Open was played every Memorial Day weekend. In 1987, it was held at Rend Lake Country Club—just off of Interstate 57, a half-hour from Southern Illinois University, where six years later I'd eventually attend. It attracted Thai golfers from across the Midwest. Since there were no age limits in each of the three divisions—men, women, and juniors—I battled against high schoolers who regularly played competitive golf, while I learned about the decimal point in sixth grade.

The night before the tournament, dark clouds lumbered in and seemed to stay over the chateau my family rented. Aunty

Sue had to work, so she stayed behind. My father watched the weather on TV, complaining about driving six hours only to have it rain, and my mother read a Thai magazine. Outside, the wind blew against the door and whistled through the tiny space underneath it. I opened the curtains and willed the weather to cease. Young trees flexed and bent in the gusts. My mother hummed "Over the Rainbow."

The weather cleared up in the early morning and a cold breeze swept through southern Illinois. The temperature hovered around fifty degrees. My father had gone to the clubhouse to see the pairings of the day. He returned stoic. "They playing by IJGA rules," he said. Illinois Junior Golf Association. "You carry own bag. Course very sloppy."

"What group am I in?"

"First group," he said.

Until then I had never carried my clubs, never walked a full eighteen holes. When my father and I practiced, we buzzed around in golf carts, which was more fun than playing. But that was farthest from my mind. My worries stemmed from the thought of hitting the first shot of the day, setting the tone and the pace of the tournament. Visions of the nightmares I had been having flashed in my head. My hands, arms, and legs felt heavy. All of a sudden, I wanted the weather to come back. I wanted the rain to pour, the wind to blow. I wished for a tornado to touch down and take me someplace that wasn't this golf course.

When I stepped onto the tee, my golf bag slung over my shoulder, I tried to ignore the crowd gathered at the first hole. It seemed everyone had stopped what they were doing to watch the first group. At school, during a session of public speaking, Mr. Turek had said if we got nervous in front of an audience to pretend they weren't there and the room was empty. I tried. I tried to imagine myself alone—only the birds and swaying trees my companions. I tried to concentrate on the first hole: slight dogleg to the right, par four, one sand trap. I tried to envision my swing, perfect and controlled, the ball exploding off my clubface, soaring down the middle of the fairway. I had the unfortunate habit, however, of following voices wherever I went. I was drawn to how people spoke, their speech patterns, the nuances in their talk. I couldn't help myself. I eavesdropped. My ears steered toward speech like magnet to metal. I was flooded in voices. "Watch him," someone to the right of me whispered. "Future star," another voice. "Ira, make your Papa proud," from behind. "Crush it," said another.

I searched for my father. I found him near a group of his friends, who wore tropical straw hats. I waved him over.

"*Mee Yai,*" he said. "You will do good."

"I'm nervous." My eyes darted from the crowd to the course to my father's chin, which, I noticed, hadn't been shaved.

"No worry," said my father. He rubbed my arms and straightened my hat. Out of all the golf videos I'd watched, all the magazines articles I'd read, nothing prepared me for this moment, nothing taught me how to rid myself of the tension that crept into my body, tightening up my back, my neck, made me yawn and want to throw up at the same time. All my father could offer was "no worry," but all I could do *was* worry.

I couldn't delay it any longer. I stuck a wooden tee into the soft ground, lining myself up to the middle of the fairway. I sent commands to every part of my body: *Hit it far. I don't care where it goes. Just get it off the ground.* As soon as I finished my thought, I brought the club back in a quick, jerky motion, my hips over-rotating. On impact, wet dirt sprayed up from the ground, staining my glasses and leaving a divot three inches behind the ball. The club barely caught it, almost a complete whiff. The ball rolled slowly into the rough ten yards in front of me.

I closed my eyes. My mother had been off to the side, under an umbrella, even though there was no rain. I heard her voice, soft and reassuring. "*Mai pen rai,*" she said. It's OK. My father looked away, sighing. I dug my hands deep into my pockets and stared straight ahead, fighting off the wetness that was clouding my vision.

After five long hours, I trudged up the eighteenth fairway. My father waited off to the side. He waved. I was too tired to return the gesture. I dragged my golf bag behind like a lagging dog. I had a miserable round. I stopped caring on the third hole and strove to be the wettest and muddiest golfer in the tournament, trudging through the deepest water puddles, jumping and splashing in them. On some holes I lost count of what I hit and tried to make up a number that sounded reasonable. By the end of the round, splotches of mud coated my yellow shirt, and the bottom half of my slacks were a darker shade of blue because they were soaked. I felt grains of soil in various parts of my body. My hair was drenched, as if I had just gotten out of the shower. The tips of my fingers were pruney, and my feet squished and squashed over the last hill and onto the green.

I took very little time with my putt. I approached and hit it. When it dropped in the hole for my only par of the day, my father cheered.

"What you shoot, *Mee Yai?*" he asked.

"One hundred and twenty-eight."

"Only one hundred twenty-eight?" He wiped away a piece a grass sticking in my hat.

"I'm tired."

He grabbed my golf bag, and I followed. My father was trying to ask me about the round, but his voice was distant in my ears, as if we had walked into a cave. The world sounded hollow. Nothing registered but my fatigue. My legs felt independent from my body. The more I willed them to work, the more they wanted to stop. Twice, I fell. The second time, my right calf cramped up. The pain made me howl. I tried to straighten my leg, but couldn't. My father knelt beside me and massaged the cramp down with his fingers. Then he told me to lean against his body as he helped me to the car. "Big strong boy," he kept saying.

The next morning, the sun streaming through the curtains, I woke up and saw a four-inch trophy by the alarm clock. My mother said I had a fever of over a hundred, and I had slept through the night under a mound of blankets. The fever didn't matter. The trophy did. The inscription on the plaque read: *Bravest Golfer.* I took it in my hands, held the gold man in my palm. Excited, I shook my father awake and asked whether the trophy was mine. Yes, he said. It was given to me at the banquet.

Years later, I learned that my father had bought the trophy long before I finished my wet round of golf. On the bottom of the white marble base was a gold label that read: *Marquette Sporting Goods, Oak Lawn, Illinois.* It was right down the street.

Practice became a chore. On short days, my father was amicable. "Ah, good shot. You hit like this, win Master soon." On other days, he spoke in hushed, harsh Thai. "Stop playing. You are terrible. Such a disgrace." He threw pebbles at me while I swung, testing my nerves and concentration. He coughed. He sneezed.

We had a routine. First: hit golf balls at the range. The goal was to hit fifteen solid shots in a row before moving on to the next club. If not, start again. On good days, I hit 165 balls, which meant I didn't hit one bad shot. On bad days, up to 500. After the driving range, we were off to the putting green to fine-tune my short game. There, I had to chip twenty balls within a five-foot radius of the hole. If not, I started over until I got it right. Next, I practiced from the sand. Same requirements. Lastly, putting, the weakest part of my game. I worked in increments. Twenty putts in a row from five feet. Five putts from ten. Two from twenty.

My father never took his eyes off me. He watched every stroke and allowed two-minute breaks between each drill. Once practice was over, it was over. He left everything that was said and done behind on the range. He carried my bag. He gave me two quarters so I could I buy a Coke. He squeezed my shoulders, which were often tight after practice. "You my big strong boy," he said. Then we loaded the car and headed home.

In 1985, *Golf Digest* rated Forest Preserve National one of the best public courses in the country. Carved through three hundred acres of Cook County Forest Preserve wood, wetland, and meadow, this gem had become our obsession. Most Saturdays, I walked on the soft fairways that felt like plush carpet under the feet. We putted on the ultra-quick greens and cursed under our breaths as the ball sped past the hole. We were surrounded by thick oaks and hickories, but tried never to hit in them. If we finished the day without hitting a ball into one of the seventy sand traps, we were lucky. We were even luckier to witness the wildlife: white-tailed deer, red foxes, beavers, muskrats, great blue herons, bluebirds, hawks, kestrels, and swallows. And when we arrived home after five hours in the sun, our skins were golden, and our golf bags were lighter because the National's ponds had swallowed up half our balls. The most beautiful thing about the National was the price. Twelve dollars a person. Ten for juniors. This was why we kept coming.

Forest National was not like other courses. My father couldn't call weeks ahead of time to reserve a spot on the weekend. If you wanted to play the National, you woke early in the morning, slept in the car until seven, and then followed the long line through the entrance of the course, grabbing a ticket from Jimmy, the course Ranger. The really crazy people sat in line as early as the evening before, making sure to get the earliest tee times and be done by the afternoon.

I looked forward to these mornings with my father. In the car, we drank Coke and talked until the sun rose and the gates opened. Sometimes my mother tagged along if she wasn't working, and it felt like a family vacation, camping on the side of the road and munching on fruit or whatever she had brought with her.

In the dark, my father was different. His words were kind and his hand made me feel secure, as if nothing would ever come between us. On the course, my father morphed into a stranger. He seldom smiled and never laughed. His face was fixed into a permanent scowl. He spoke Thai words my mother never wanted me to learn. I found it difficult negotiating between my father's two personalities, and because of this, I questioned my golfing abilities and self-worth, which had become entangled in each other. Every shot had to be pure. If not, he'd make me feel as if I had wronged him.

Deep into the summer, before leaving Harnew Elementary for Simmons Middle School, at the National, I had had to pee since the third hole, and Kyle, the person we were paired with, said he saw a snake in the woods, said it almost bit his dick off. Even though I was twelve, I was still naive about most things and believed that somewhere in the Illinois Forest Preserve there was a cobra slithering in the woods, looking for dicks.

That day my father criticized my every hit—bad or good. Everything I did displeased him. When I missed an easy putt, he sighed and moaned. He threw his club on the cart path, the metal driver scraping on the concrete, blaming his anger on my ugly swing.

"Stop play and waste my money. You never good."

The longer the day went on, the more I had to pee. I started hitting without aiming. Putting without reading the line. I quickened my pace from shot to shot. Kyle thought I was skipping when I walked. By the sixteenth hole, my hands started to shake and I felt flashes of hot and cold. I didn't want to tell my father I had to pee. I didn't want to say a thing to him, afraid of being lashed out at.

So on the par three seventeenth hole, 205 yards, a large black pond guarding the front of the green, I lined up to the target and peed my pants. I peed and no one noticed. No one saw my pants turn a darker shade of black. My father and Kyle watched my ball fly over the water, speeding like a bullet. They watched it skitter off the pond's surface, bouncing once, twice, three times before making the leap over a log barrier and nearly rolling into the hole.

It was a shot you'd talk about the rest of your life, one that would make you believe in the divine. Certainly, it was my father's favorite story. He told it with great vigor. He reenacted my swing. He made his hand zoom like a golf ball. He exaggerated. The ball no longer bounced three times off the water, but seven, hitting the flagstick and jumping out of the hole. But for me, the shot only brought embarrassment and anger toward my father for not telling me it was OK to pee in the woods.

"Shit," Kyle said. "That was fuckin' beautiful."

I whispered a thank you and walked back to the golf cart.

"*Tee dee*," my father said. Hit good. It was the first good comment he had made all day, but I was past feeling good.

"Lucky," he said. "Good player always have luck."

I turned away from him and shrugged.

On rare occasions, my mother and Aunty Sue tagged along on our golfing adventures. They played to be outdoors, to get away from the confines of the house and the hospital. It was also a chance for us to do something as a family, which had become less frequent since my mother and aunt changed hospitals.

They weren't serious golfers. They giggled like schoolgirls and displayed improper golfing etiquette: shouting to one another from across the fairway; stubbornly sitting by ponds, scavenging for lost balls; forgetting to replace divots and rake sand traps. Both of them had uncontrollable bladders. Sometimes, they'd tell me to stand guard as they piddled behind the golf cart, their asses hanging out of their slacks.

They both amused and embarrassed me. "God, you guys are so childish."

"Not God," said my aunt. "Buddha."

"Don't talk like that," my mother said.

I stuck out my tongue and she chased me around the course with her driver.

My mother was the worse of the two. Here was a woman who feared and distrusted America, who often tried to hide and never call attention to herself, who on the golf course played Catch-A-Fart, a game where you farted into your hand and either threw it into your opponent's face, or for the ultimate win, you gas masked your opponent's mouth and nose. There was something about the green fairways, the trees, the openness of a golf course that allowed my mother to shed her inhibition and become the ultimate brat. Whatever it was, her presence, Aunty Sue's presence, was a welcome change to my and my father's routine.

When they were along, my father never showed his other side. He remained quiet and smiled at their antics. He offered tips to both of them. Aunty Sue took them graciously; my mother told him to be quiet.

Perhaps it was the early-morning drive that upset my father that day, or the constant backseat driving my mother did, or last week's tournament where I played terribly and came in second, but when we arrived at Silver Lakes Country Club in Palos Hills, he made family time into practice. On the sixth hole, he grabbed my ball and whipped it into the pond, saying he would make things easier for me.

Neither my mother nor my aunt had ever seen our practices; they had never known what went on during the weekend. I never told them because no matter what my father did or said, I still wanted to be with him, still wanted to be the golfer he wanted me to be, still believed I could be that golfer.

After nine holes, we took a small break to eat lunch. Aunty Sue packed individual meals—fried rice and a fried egg for me and *kai phad ped,* spicy chicken, for everyone else. She had wrapped our lunches tightly in foil and kept them out of the sun. She passed out our packets of food, and I sat on the ground, brushing army ants off my lap, spooning rice and egg into my mouth. My mother chomped down on a stalk of green onion. My father waited for his packet.

"*Tatane, lurm,*" Aunty Sue said. Oh goodness, I forgot your lunch. She offered to give him money for a hot dog, but my father shrugged, wiping his sweaty brow, and told her he'd buy one for himself.

Compared to Aunty Sue's food, a golf course hot dog was a piece of turd wrapped in bread and my father knew it. He ate it slowly, moving his lips in disdain. Mustard spilled onto his shirt, and he cursed in Thai. He asked my mother for a bit of hers, but she simply ignored him, as if he were an annoying spirit in her ear. She hadn't spoken to him since the second hole, her anger spilling over into silence. He asked me for a bite of my food, but I had inhaled mine in minutes.

Aunty Sue did not forget my father's lunch like she had told him. On the eleventh hole, when my father went to pee in the woods, she and my mother drove up next to me and handed me my father's lunch. "Look thin today," my mother said evenly, even though I was almost five nine and close to two hundred pounds, even though she was always on me about my weight. "Eat," she said. "All."

Aunty Sue winked and mouthed, *quickly.*

On the sixteenth hole, my mother and aunt reached their limit. My father tossed a golf ball at me while I was in midswing, something he often did. He wanted me to be focused on the ball I was about to hit. Even if a bomb were to fall and decimate the world, he'd say, I should still manage to hit a perfect shot. Though I was sure he didn't mean it, this time the ball he tossed hit my glasses and knocked out one of the lenses. Suddenly half-sighted, I jerked up, the speed of my swing disrupted. I sprayed the ball fifty yards to the left.

"*So lur lur,*" said my father, which was his way of saying "error," the syllables distinct. He drove away, while I fumbled around with my glasses, trying to pop the lens back in.

From across the fairway, my mother and Aunty Sue witnessed the entire scene. Even with my blurred vision, I saw them turn and whisper to each other. The lens refused to go back in, so I took off my glasses and shoved them in my pocket.

My father was ahead of us all. In golf, it was common courtesy to stay together, never moving ahead before your playing partners hit. Common courtesy. Safety, also. My father sometimes left me behind to show how displeased he was with my game. He was about seventy-five yards away, off to the right, nowhere near my mother's line of shot. When she was about to hit, I noticed her body wasn't lined up to the target. I told her so, but she muttered something I couldn't understand and hit. She was dead on. When you hit a good shot, you don't have to look at it; you just know where the ball will end up. My mother turned away and put the club into her bag. She hit a screamer that sped toward my father, who had his back to us. I could've yelled a warning. I could've told my father to duck. I kept quiet. I watched the ball connect with my father's back. He threw his arms and shoulders back. He screamed, a guttural sound. He tried to grab the place where my mother hit him, but it was out of reach of his fingers. He danced back and forth, teetering on one leg, then the other.

"*Arai wah?*" he said, his voice loud and whiny. What the hell? "Why don't you be careful?!"

My mother shrugged. "Why you get in way of ball?" she said.

"It hurts," he said.

"It will bruise," said my aunt, stating the obvious.

I smiled.

I finished the last three holes with a birdie and two pars, despite my impaired vision. My father was in too much pain to continue. He followed along in the golf cart, telling us all how much it hurt, how he felt like there was a ball stuck in him. No one listened. At the last green, my mother smothered her stinky hand over my nose. I gasped dramatically. Aunty Sue holed a ten-footer for par, and we ended the round laughing.

My father's back *was* bruised. More than bruised. When he took his shirt off there was a golf ball-sized welt in the center of his back like a tumor. I wanted to touch it.

As soon as I got home, I called Mike and Kevin, telling them about my father's tumor-like bruise. I told them it was bigger than it really was. I told them it moved like the creature that popped out of that dude's stomach in the movie *Alien.*

My father knocked on my bedroom door. I was reading a comic book. When he came in, he looked older than I had ever seen him. I often forgot my father was not a young father. He was fifty-five, as old as some grandparents, though he appeared to be forty, thirty-eight even. In the light of the room, though, his wrinkles were deep and the outsides of his eyes were a misty cream. There was a visible streak of white through the right side of his hair, which I had never noticed before. He winced with each step.

"Does your back still hurt?"

He nodded.

"Is it still big?" I set the comic down on my bed and moved over so he could sit.

He shook his head and sat on the edge of my bed, his knees facing the other direction, as if at any moment he would pop up and leave. "*Fung Pau nah . . .*" he said quietly. Listen to me . . ."

"I am sorry."

I was taken by surprise and said the only thing that came to me. "I think I need new glasses. The lens doesn't want to stay in." I showed him the Scotch tape I had put on the frame.

"OK," he said, turning toward me. "Are you mad?"

"No," I said.

"Sad?"

I shrugged.

He took my glasses from me and inspected them.

He smiled and told me he would never be like that again. He only wanted the best for me and sometimes he was blinded by his eagerness. He looked at the glasses again, and said they were easy to fix. All it needed was a new screw and some tightening. He left the room, and a few minutes later, he brought back my glasses, fixed and cleaned, like brand new.

Part Two

You know yourself
what wounds is the same
for all of us.

—"Childhood: A Portrait," Katherine Riegel

Haunted Trails

In 1984, Wat Dhammaram moved to the outskirts of Bridge-view, a suburb ten minutes away from our house. The new temple was surrounded by a public park, a truck-yard, and across the street, a whole residential area that did not want us there. The building had once been an elementary school. The windows were cracked and cardboarded, cockroaches infested the bathrooms, and stray cats made homes in old drawers and closets. Though the monks meant to clean up the *wat* as quickly as possible, transform it into the Thai Buddhist Mecca of the Midwest, some neighbors prevented that by adding new cracks to new windows and egg stains to just-washed doors. At night, they blew up quarter sticks of dynamite, making craters in the gravel parking lot. We filled in the craters and replaced the windows without complaint.

Despite the first few years of uneasiness our Sundays continued like normal. The old toothless woman still barbequed Thai chicken; monks taught Buddhism; sermons bored me to tears; and Simon was still Simon.

In the fall, after classes, many of the boys played football. Simon was always one of the captains because he brought the ball, and I was picked second to last, even though I believed I was the best player on the field. With my friends at Harnew, it took four or five of them to bring me down, and once at Keith Kavalauskaus's birthday party, I pulled the whole opposing team across the touchdown line to cheers from siblings and parents.

"Here's one end," Simon said. He pointed to a small baby tree. "And the other touchdown is the sidewalk." We played in the front lawn of the *wat* because the monks had planted ten trees equidistance from one another, our first-down markers. Across the street, beyond a ten-foot fence, white teenagers began gathering at a house with junk strewn all over the front yard. We ignored them.

"Who's the other captain?" Den asked. Den was a scrawny kid with a big head. Sometimes I imagined him floating away, his head full of helium.

"Ira," said Simon with a cocky smile. "I like his new shoes."

"Shut up," I said, embarrassed of my Pro-wings bought at Payless.

"You pick first, tough guy," Simon said.

"Sampan," I said without hesitation.

Sampan stood apart from everyone else. He was on the big side, like me, his cheeks like a squirrel carrying nuts. His hair was so dark it reflected light. He never joined in on Simon's jeering. He never said much of anything. In classes, he listened intently and wrote copious notes. His mother made him play football with us, instead of hiding in the library. Usually, he played with his hands in his pockets, walking out into the field, never expecting anything. Most of the time the other boys treated him like a ghost. But I knew Sampan could play. I watched him toss a Nerf football high in the air and catch it. He had good hands.

It was gray out, and the flags on the poles quivered in the breeze. There were three of them—the red, white, and blue of Thailand, the red, white, and blue of USA, and the canary yellow Buddhist flag. A few girls sat at a picnic table at the other end of the field. We won the toss and were heading in that direction.

"Throw it to me," Imsorn said. Imsorn was girl-obsessed.

In our huddle I outlined patterns on my palm and told each of my teammates what route they should take. "Got it?" They nodded.

"And me?" Imsorn said.

"Toward the girls."

We lined up. Simon stood in front of me. He was a rusher and had to count till eight before he could charge the quarterback, me. When I hiked the ball, I peddled back quickly and released the ball down the field to Imsorn, who outran his man. Simon grabbed me and tried to take me down, but I was too big and shrugged him off. The football landed softly in Imsorn's waiting hands. Touchdown.

Imsorn danced in the end zone. The Robot. Then flexed. The girls rolled their eyes.

From across the fence, the group of teenage boys hooted. "Nice throw, big guy," one of them said. "He's a regular Favre," said another. We ignored them.

When it was Simon's turn on offense, he threw a low screamer. I tipped the pass and the ball wobbled into Sampan's hand, an interception that turned into another touchdown.

Simon rarely lost. He was losing against me, my team, which included Sampan, who everyone assumed was the worst player. Simon grabbed the Nerf football and began squeezing it like an accordion. Then with a scream, he chucked it out of temple grounds and across the street. He regretted it as soon as he did it, cursing under his breath. One of the boys on the other side of the fence ran over and got the ball.

"This is a pretty ball," the kid said. It was. It was hot pink and black.

"Give it back." Simon said.

The white boys started playing with Simon's football. We watched silently. There was nothing we could do. We were afraid of them. We were afraid of what they would do to us, to our family, to the monks, to the temple. We were together in our powerlessness, and it was a rare moment. I felt part of the Thai community, watching these boys toss our ball around. All of us stood clustered together, wordless.

Simon pouted at the fence, his fingers through the chain link. At one point, he looked as if he were going to climb over and steal his ball back. Instead he said, "You win," and then headed inside the temple.

I wasn't sure whether he said it to me or the boys, who started a game of their own, pretending we weren't there under the same gray sky, no more then thirty feet away. Soon, one-by-one, our players followed Simon back into the temple. Imsorn jogged over to the girls at the picnic table and started flirting. Sampan and I continued to watch the game.

"You beat Simon," Sampan said, a shy smile sneaked across his lips.

"I guess," I said.

"You're way better than that kid." Sampan pointed at a boy who chucked an incomplete pass. The ball wobbled in the air, crashing on the concrete, rolling into a yard of tall grass.

I was addicted to Sampan, the way Mike was addicted to vampires and all things mysterious, the way Kevin was addicted to sport cars. I talked about my Thai friend constantly. I bragged about his artistic ability. Sampan was a year older, officially a teenager, while I still piddled around in the seventh grade.

On Sundays, we sat next to each other in class. Sampan's pen never stopped. What I had thought were copious notes on suffering were actually expert drawings of comic book heroes of his own creation. In between his doodles were notes here and there about Buddha's teachings.

During lunch, we hid in Sampan's gold and rusted Cadillac and talked about girls. Girls had become something more than the annoying other sex; they were the annoying other sex I wanted to spend time with.

"You've kissed a girl?" Sampan asked, exasperated and amazed.

"Two," I said. "On the lips." Actually, it had been one girl on the cheek, and it wasn't really a kiss, more like I tripped and fell on her face.

"What was it like?"

"I don't know," I said. "Warm."

"Who were they?"

I blurted out the names of the two most popular girls in Simmons Middle School. "Madeline and Tanya."

"You kissed two girls!" He stuck out his hand. "Man, are you the coolest or what?"

"The coolest," I said and shook it.

With Sampan, I'd often bragged about how wonderful I was at everything, impressing him with my talents. He had such patience with me, listening attentively to whatever I said, never questioning my stories even when I made most things up. I was becoming more and more like my father, a storyteller. Lies came easily to me and without thought. I'd open my mouth, and suddenly, I had wrestled a boar to the ground in the jungles of Thailand or I had met Eddie Murphy at Wisconsin Dells or I had kissed two girls.

Sampan was much more talented than I could ever be, which was why I bragged and lied and pretended to be someone I was not. I envied his gift of art, his perfect drawings. I envied his quick brain and the straight A's he received on his report card. I envied his Thai name.

Sampan's parents had divorced. This was a surprising detail. Divorce was common with my white friends. Harnew parents were getting divorced left and right. Kevin's parents were on the rocks. Mike's parents split, and he and his little sister stayed at the house most of the week and at his mother's apartment on weekends. For a long time, divorce seemed an American concept. My mother had been warning me about Americans, how they easily loved, how you couldn't trust them, how at any moment they could leave you stranded and find someone else. She always followed with how I should find a nice Thai girl, who would be devoted only to me. In this regard, I believed my mother, believed that in the aspects of love, Thais were superior, were immune to divorce.

Sampan's father lived somewhere on the West Coast. He never liked to talk about his father, but I knew he was never far from Sampan's mind. Once I said he looked like him from a picture. Sampan punched me in the arm so hard it bruised, the only time he was ever physical with me. The subject of his father never came up again.

"Your dad's so cool," Sampan said once. We lay on the hood of his car. It was the Thai New Year, mid-April, and the *wat* was having its yearly celebration. Thai music vibrated from within its walls, the *aw*, a xylophone-like instrument, screeched on tight cords.

"He's all right," I said.

"What do you mean, 'he's all right'?"

"He's just my dad."

"Whatever."

"What's up?" I said.

"Nothing," he said.

I envied his heart the most, how tears fell easily for him.

At the back of the *wat*, outside the activities room where boys took Thai boxing lessons and girls learned how to Thai dance, hung a bulletin board of young Thai achievements: short articles about high school tennis stars who qualified for the state tournament; a small blurb about a violin virtuoso who got a full ride to Harvard; and at the center of the bulletin board this week was a newspaper photo of me, teeing off at Glenview Golf Club.

Sampan and I stood in front of the bulletin board. It was lunchtime, ten minutes before afternoon classes. I hated the picture. I looked like a fat oaf.

My father couldn't contain himself. He bought twenty copies of *The Star* and distributed them to people at temple, and when he ran out, he made thirty Xerox copies of the article. The clipping wasn't only tacked onto the achievement board, but other bulletin boards around the temple. Wherever I walked, there I was, looking into the distance, my eyes following my drive. On one of the pictures, I found a mustache penned over my face, and a comic book bubble that read: "Hi, I'm big and fat." It didn't take long to figure out who had done it.

"The two nerds," Simon said from behind. He had dark sunglasses and jeans with stylish holes in them. Over the years, Simon had gotten taller, slimmer, his face losing some of its boyhood puffiness. Many of the girls, especially the older high schoolers, babied him, and he snuggled up to their chests. To Sampan and me, he was the devil child.

Sampan dug deep into his pockets and slouched; he often did when Simon was around. I crossed my arms and tried to look tough.

"I'm so tired of seeing your face," Simon said.

"You're such a geek," I said.

"Nice comeback," he said. "Do you play golf because you can stroke it a lot?" He made an up and down motion with his hand.

"Whatever," I said. I turned to Sampan, who stared at his feet.

"Oh my god," Simon started laughing, "you have no clue what I'm talking about, do you?"

"You're stupid," I said.

"Blow each other," Simon said. He dribbled the basketball down the hall, smirking. Then he stopped and turned. "Do you know what *that* means?" He laughed again and went into the classroom. I glared at where he used to be and gave him the finger.

"I hate him," I mumbled.

"Me too," Sampan said.

The thought of staying another minute in class filled me with dread. "Let's get the hell out of here," I said. "I can't take another second of this place, another second of, of . . . that asshole."

"That's the whole point," Sampan said. "Suffering." He mocked our new Buddhism teacher, a monk with alien eyes, a monk who spoke about suffering 24/7.

Phra Ajahn Wangkran, my favorite teacher, had become a man again. His hair grew in thickly, and he kept a goatee. In the hallways I would greet him, sometimes calling him my holy teacher, but he would remind me that he was no longer Phra Ajahn. It was disconcerting to see him in jeans and a button down shirt. For a long time, gossip flew in every direction—he found a woman, he was thinking unholy thoughts. After some time, he stopped coming to temple and I never heard about him again.

"Come on," I said. "If I stay here, I'm going to die."

"Where?" Sampan asked.

"Haunted Trails."

Part of him, I knew, felt obligated to be a good Thai student. The other part was already at Haunted Trails—an entertainment park with mini golf, go-karts, batting cages, and arcades, Sampan's ultimate weakness.

Finally, he nodded.

We made it outside without anyone asking where we were headed. Then we went around the fence into Nottingham Park. At the far corner, the chain-link had been cut and we squeezed through. There was a curvy trail, most likely made by neighborhood kids. The grass along the trampled trail went up to our knees.

I told Sampan I heard there was a secret gang that owned this territory, the White Dragons, so we had to be cool or we'd get our asses cut. Sampan asked if I made this up and I told him hell no. I told him I heard other kids talk about them. They were a bunch of white kids who wore white bandanas around their white heads. I told him they carried switchblades in their back pockets.

Sampan's eyes widened and darted from sound to sound.

I thought about what Simon had said. Stroking and blowing. I didn't know what he meant, but I figured it was dirty and sexual. At twelve, everything was dirty and sexual. I wanted to ask Sampan, but I stopped on the trail, staring ahead. In the distance, a gang of boys made their way toward us. One was sucking on a lollipop. Sampan whispered, "White Dragons." I told him to be cool. I told him to get behind me and let them pass. Even though Sampan and I were bigger than these kids, they outnumbered us, five to two. One of the boys had spiked hair. Other than that, they looked similar. I wondered if they were brothers. When they saw us, they slowed, too, and formed a line of their own. We passed each other silently.

When we were out of the possibility of trouble, Sampan turned and asked, "Why do you hate us?"

"What are you doing?" I pulled at the cuff of his shirt.

One of the kids, the oldest, I assumed, said, "What are you talking about?"

"You blow up the driveway. You throw rocks at our monks."

The kid turned to look at his friends—half-smiling, half-laughing—as if to say, *what is this dude on?* "We didn't do any of that," he said. I stood behind Sampan, my hands fists, ready to throw down and protect my best friend, who didn't know how to fight, who was getting us in a lot of trouble.

"Jesus, Sam," I nudged.

"Listen," the boy said. He took a step toward us, and I took a step toward him. "We didn't do any of that shit. We don't care whether you're there or not. A lot of them hate you. But we're not them."

Sampan smiled and stuck out his hand. "Thanks," he said.

The kid looked at it for a moment. But he shook it anyway, and I took a deep breath. "Later," the boy said, and turned away, leading his group back into Nottingham.

I punched Sampan in the arm. "What in the hell were you thinking?"

"I wasn't," he said. "I don't know."

"You're a dick." But what I meant was: you're the bravest person I've ever met.

We continued walking to Haunted Trails and spent the afternoon inserting tokens into graphic fighting machines. We made sure to get back to the *wat* before class let out, so our parents wouldn't know we ditched. Sampan and I sneaked into the temple and hid in the library, which was being remodeled. It was next door to our class. I wanted to know what the Phra Ajahn was saying through the wall. I pressed my ear to it. Sampan took a seat and brought out his notebook to doodle.

"Is he saying anything new?" Sampan asked.

The voice was muffled, but I was able to hear a few phrases. "He's saying everyone suffers," I reported back. "When do we stop?"

If the point of Buddhism was cause and effect, if we were to believe that we had hundreds of paths, each leading us toward a vague something, if we truly had the power of decision to alleviate suffering, then Haunted Trails was our answer. Sampan and I, indeed, suffered. We suffered in Simon's presence; we suffered from boredom; we suffered from classes about suffering. We chose to lessen our anguish by taking the path farthest from the *wat,* one that cut through the tall grass and snaked toward the giant-sized Frankenstein in the distance, even in

sacrifice of the teachings of Buddha, because to us, enlightenment was the rush and thrill of defeating *Samurai Showdown.*

I returned home one Sunday around six. My mother and
aunt worked nights and usually went to bed at four in the afternoon and woke at nine.

Today, they were awake. Today, they waited.

"What you learning?" asked my aunt. She wore old hospital
scrubs she recycled as sleepwear.

"Same thing," I said.

"Tell us," said my mother. She sat on the stairs leading up to
the bedroom in her satin night gown, with pink rollers in her
hair.

I tried to recall anything from language classes that morning, anything from the morning sermon. What raced through
my mind, though, were scenes from arcade games: a hero
hacking enemies to bits, a racecar speeding toward the finish
line, a ghostly gun shooting at cowboys dressed in black.

"We went over vowels again," I said.

"Recite," said my aunt.

I did, all thirty-two of them. I had known my vowels since I
was in first grade.

"How about Buddhism?" my mother asked.

"Buddha's pretty cool," I said.

"You learn about Triple Gem?" asked my mother.

"Yeah," I said. "Exactly."

"What they are?" said my aunt, leaning against the entryway
of the kitchen, smiling slyly.

The Triple Gem. It was a guiding principle of Buddhism like
the Father, Son, and Holy Ghost in Christianity, only here it
was Buddha, Dharma (Buddha's teachings), and Sangha (his
disciples). I had forgotten it, standing nervously in front of
my mother and aunt, searching around in my memory, sifting
through all the days and years of learning about Buddhism,

trying to remember one morsel of Buddhist fact, but all had blurred into one big blank spot. It was as if Buddha himself had entered my mind and put his hand over my brain.

I couldn't meet their eyes. "Triple Gem," I said. "They were the rocks Buddha found on the shore of a river before he gained enlightenment."

Aunty Sue laughed.

"What is the fourth precept?" my mother asked in Thai, her scowl deep.

This I knew. "Not to lie," I said.

"Good Thai boy do not lying," she said.

Another nod.

Aunty Sue moved to touch my cheek and I squirmed away from her fingers. I used to relish any touch from my parents, loved my father's hand on my shoulder, my mother's kiss on the forehead, and Aunty Sue's tight embrace. Now, I wanted to separate myself from them. I felt uncomfortable with their touch because to be cuddled was to be young. I wasn't young anymore.

My aunt laughed again. "Not boy. Man. Voice like man. Tall like man."

"Man still love Buddha," said my mother. "You thinking of girl?"

Almost every minute, I wanted to say. I thought about Tanya's dimpled smile. I thought about Madeline's long lashes. I thought about Brenda's boobs and Karen's legs. I thought about Kristen's hair and the small mole on Diane's left arm.

Worst of all, I loved white girls, who, in my mother's mind, were the quintessential evil in America. All over my bedroom walls I had posters of white girls smiling seductively and wearing skimpy bikinis. I was on the phone with girls for hours. They consumed my nighttime dreams, and when I woke up, they were everywhere with their high hair and bellybuttonrevealing blouses. Blondes, redheads, brunettes—it didn't matter because I loved them all—Lind, Murphy, Sherwood, Doran, Pine, such glorious Anglo last names! They had artificially tanned skin, pointy European noses, and round eyes.

I told my mother no. I didn't think about girls.

"Do you dream about girl?" asked my aunt.

My dreamworld had begun to blend the child and the boy, between play and desire. The dream I remembered most, the one that often recurred, was a falling dream. Here, I teetered on a pole that extended high in the sky, past layers and layers of clouds, extending into space and the stars. I knew I would fall. I knew I would come crashing down to earth. Usually, I woke before the crash, but now, when the interplanetary wind pushed the pole over and I tipped into the Earth's atmosphere, a screaming fireball, I saw on each passing cloud angels. Supermodel angels. *Sports Illustrated* swimsuit angels. They waved and blew me kisses. My fall slowed to a halt, and I extended my hand toward them, and I was not worried anymore about crashing and dying. I was not worried about anything. Just when my fingers were about to graze skin I woke in a sweat. I woke breathless.

"No," I said. "Girls suck."

Once a month, Mike, Kevin and I planned sleepovers at each other's houses. This month, Mike was grounded for yelling at his baby sister and couldn't make it to Kevin's, which was the ultimate place for a sleepover. His house was twice the size of mine. His room was in the basement where there was a fully stocked kitchen, four arcade games, and a big TV. Kevin also had a waterbed, which we sometimes sat on to tell ghost stories, the undulations of the bed making us feel adrift and lost.

Kevin's mother dropped us off at Video Den, while she went to the grocery store next door. We perused what videos we wanted to watch for the hundredth time: *Poltergeist,* though I hated horror movies, or Cheech Marin's *Born in East L.A.* In the back of Video Den was a room closed off from the rest of the store. Above swinging doors was a sign that read "No One Under 21 Allowed."

Kevin and I stood in Action films, a few steps from the forbidden room. He grabbed a Van Damme movie, but wasn't looking at the box. His eyes settled on the door. Mine, too, though I was pretending to check out *Fist of Fury.* He put Van Damme back down and darted for the doors before I could say anything.

I followed, but stopped short. I grabbed the closest video box without looking at the title. "You're gonna get caught," I whispered.

Kevin didn't reply. I looked left and right, making sure no one was headed our way. Video Den was slow at that hour. There was only a woman who worked the counter, but she was busy sorting returned videos.

"What do you see?" I kept my voice under the hum of the air conditioner.

"Dude," Kevin said. "You gotta come in here."

His hand emerged through the door. He grabbed my T-shirt and pulled me in. I turned away. It was a reflex. Whenever I watched a movie with my mother or father and a boob happened to come on screen, they always told me to close my eyes, and for extra protection, they placed their hands over my face. But they weren't here. I opened one eye and then the other and then opened them wider. There they were, shelves and shelves of naked or nearly naked women, women staring at me, giving me a feeling I had never felt before, a tightening in my stomach—no, it wasn't there—it was lower, and it wasn't a tightening sensation exactly, it was pulsating, it was rhythmic, it was a drumbeat, only I wasn't just hearing it, but feeling it resonate throughout my body like a pebble dropped in water, the ripples spreading and spreading and spreading, and my fingertips, yes, they were feeling it, and my toes, there too, and in the tips of my earlobes, they quivered, they shook.

Kevin grabbed a box and turned it over. Men and women. Entangled in awkward positions. Stars covering the most revealing parts.

Kevin and I existed outside of time. Inside this small cubical room, we were separated from the world where things made some sense. This was the rabbit hole Alice fell through. This was what lay behind the secret door in the hedge. And suddenly, I had to leave. Kevin, too. He put the box down, and we walked through the door and past the counter to the outside where we sat on the sidewalk and waited for Kevin's mother to pick us up.

"What did you think?" he said. He wasn't looking at me, but straight ahead at the Cicero traffic.

It was frighteningly lovely. It was repulsive. It was beyond imagination.

"Cool," I said.

"Way cool," said Kevin.

My mother was delighted I finally found a Thai friend. It meant I was mixing with people of my own culture—smart and ambitious, who knew to take off their shoes before entering the house, who wanted to be doctors, lawyers, engineers, and businessmen. These were the occupations of choice for first generation Thai Americans. Indeed, Sampan planned on becoming a doctor.

Through osmosis, my mother had hoped I'd become smarter by hanging around a superb student like Sampan. I began getting B's and C's. I hardly did any of my homework because I was thinking about three things: 1) Sampan, 2) boobs, 3) golf. Because my mother and aunt worked nights, they couldn't monitor my schoolwork like before. From four to nine, while they slept, I watched TV; talked to Sampan, Mike, or Kevin on the phone; played Nintendo; and ate junk food. My schedule was full.

I was afraid, though, to bring home my report cards and show my mother that the only A I received was in gym. The rest hovered around average. During my first quarter in eighth grade, I began practicing the elegant curve of my mother's signature. Her handwriting was an example of perfect penmanship. There wasn't anything fancy in her letters, not like my father's crazy looking M, or Aunty's Sue's snake-like scribble. My mother's signature was beautifully standard. I practiced it over and over in a notebook. Once I perfected it, I burned the notebook, destroying the evidence, because my mother was known to check for suspicious trash.

When my homeroom teacher, Mr. Himmelman, sent me home with my report card, I took off across 95th Street to the Chicago Ridge Mall and used their public copy machine. I made a copy of the original, white-ed out my grades, made another copy, and then filled it out with different letters. I never gave myself straight A's, though the temptation was always there. I knew if I had brought all A's home, my mother and aunt would have bought me whatever I asked for. Still, I resisted the urge. I didn't want to tip off my mother. There was a certain thrill in being nearly perfect.

My deception worked every time. Eventually, I believed Aunty Sue caught on. She said things like: "Must be so smart. Never bring any book home to study," or, "All teacher have same writing." No matter her doubts, she never told my mother.

Because of our friendship, my family adopted Sampan's family. My mother and Aunty Sue took in Tasanee like a sister. They talked on the phone, exchanging temple gossip. Tasanee filled them in on what they had missed. When my mother and aunt were able to make it to temple, the three of them sat next to each other, listening intently to the sermon, nodding their collective heads, folding their hands at almost the same time.

Aunty Sue made Thai desserts—sticky rice with sweet custard, *sungkaya,* or sweet honey squash—and sent it with me to give it to Sampan's mother.

Even closer friends were my father and Tasanee. Where one went, the other followed. Because Tasanee was in charge of putting together lunches for students after the morning session, my father chipped in by picking up the large orders of White Castle hamburgers or Thai fried rice at restaurants. When they weren't working, they could be found talking and laughing in the kitchen with other parents.

Tasanee wore the same thing every Sunday: a long dark dress that looked like what Texan women wore when they went line dancing. She over-powdered her face. Up close I could see the cracks in her make-up. She traced her lips in vivid red. Her hair was frizzy and wide. She kept a close eye on Sampan.

I had the feeling she distrusted me. I believed she thought I was leading her son astray.

Tasanee was not wrong. I *was* leading Sampan astray. I suggested bad boy things: ditch class, lie, stand up to his mother, value material things and girls over his education. Sampan argued more about the clothes she made him wear, about the amount of money she didn't spend on him. Sampan's grades were slipping—from A's to A-'s. And sadly, he was lovesick with a pretty Jewish girl who didn't know he existed.

The afternoon after Kevin's sleepover, Sampan and I were at temple. I told Sampan about the secret room at Video Den. I told him about the naked women. I told him next week Kevin invited us to his house to watch *Summer Slam,* a World Wrestling Federation pay-per-view event, except his father didn't pay for it because he had a scrambler that stole channels.

Sampan got out his notebook of drawings. He began to sketch a woman, starting from the bottom up, legs long and lean, stomach flat and toned. When he got to her chest, he said, "How big?"

"Big," I said, cupping the foot of air in front of me.

We sat in the library. Boxes of Buddhist books were scattered across the floor. On the walls of the classroom were pictures of the King and venerable monks. They seemed to watch what these two boys were doing, seemed to judge from above. We didn't care.

When Sampan finished the drawing, he asked, "What should we call her?"

"Boob Girl," I said. Boob Girl hovered in the white of the paper. She wore a tight body suit that hugged the curves of her hips and breasts. She had rich black hair, the strands of which fell over her eyes, and from her fingers were sparks of electricity.

"What's her power?" I said.

"She can blast you with her fingers," Sampan said. "And, with a stare, she can turn you into ice. Last year, in class, I read about Medusa, who turned men into stone. Only she was ugly. Had snakes in her hair. But Boob Girl, she's so beautiful guys freeze up."

I felt that way about a few girls at Simmons.

"This is your best drawing yet, Sam."

"Nah." He put the notebook back into his book bag.

"It is."

"Nothing special," he said.

"Shut up." I rose from my chair and got a thumbtack from a bulletin board. Sampan and I had bought two cans of sodas from a vending machine. He liked orange soda. I liked grape. I poked a hole into the top of my can, shook it up, and sprayed Sampan. The carbonation forced the soda to shoot out in a tiny stream. "Say it's your best work."

"No," said Sampan.

I squirted him again.

Sampan ran to the bulletin board to get a tack to poke into his can. From then on, it was shoot or be shot. We ran around the library squirting each other, spraying the books, the tables, the walls, the pictures, the ceiling fan spinning above us, the glass cabinets that protected the rarest Buddhist books, our hair, our faces, our backs. I aimed for his glasses, ducking in and out of chairs, pretending to be the ultra-suave James Bond. Sampan lurked around corners, a cop on a drug bust. We were sticky. We were laughing hard.

In mid-spray, Tasanee thundered into the room. "What are you doing?"

Sampan froze, his finger over the hole in the can, stopping the stream. I tried to hide in the corner. She yanked the can out of Sampan's hand, and a bit of the pop squirted up at her face, which was red and puffy like a bee had stung her. The can dented in her grip.

She grabbed a fistful of Sampan's white dress shirt with purple streaks all over it. "Who did this?" she finally said.

I hid the can behind my back. Sampan looked down at his soda-speckled shoes.

"Who?" she said again. She raised her eyes and saw me in the corner. Her mouth twitched, and I could feel the words pressing against her lips, all the things she wanted to say but held back. I wanted to look away, but didn't.

After a few long seconds, she stormed out of the room, banging the door behind her.

Sampan took a seat and looked at his fingers. "I'm sticky."

I was still in the corner, frozen. "She hates me," I said.

"She just thinks I can do better."

I stared at him, mouth open.

"Kidding," he said and laughed.

I kept Sampan separate from Mike and Kevin. I talked about Sampan to them, talked about them to Sampan, but I was hesitant to have them mingle. I feared the meeting of these two worlds would be catastrophic. I feared they'd hate each other and I'd be stuck in the middle and would have to choose who I'd rather be with, which ultimately meant what world I'd rather exist in. For so long, I had lived two lives. During the week, I was Ira the white kid. I played volleyball and was on the track team. I goofed around with two white kids, who spent most of their days talking about comics or Nintendo. On weekends, I was Ira the Thai. I played football with other Thais, ditched classes with my best Thai friend. But these friends wanted to meet. They wanted to hang out. So when Kevin mentioned watching *Summer Slam* at his house, I said OK.

When Sampan and I entered the house, Mike and Kevin were playing Techmo Football on the big-screen TV. Bonww Jovi blared from stereo speakers, singing some sappy love song I secretly liked but made sure to say it sucked in public. Mike and Kevin introduced themselves and Sampan asked if he could join in. They got along immediately, talking smack back and forth, pressing buttons on the game controllers and high-fiving each other. Pretty soon, they were picking up each other's lingoes. Mike and Kevin started saying "salty." Sampan used "gnarly" and "rad" a few times.

After an hour, I noticed the house was empty, only us boys. "Where are your mom and dad?" I asked Kevin.

"They went to the store to get pizza, pop and stuff," he said.

Mike put the game on pause. He wore an oversized denim bandanna that made him look like a mini pirate. "Kevin has something to show us."

"Totally," Kevin said. "I almost forgot." He turned off the Nintendo and pressed play on the VCR.

On the TV, there was a naked woman lying on her back, and a naked man on top of her. She screamed, but not a horror movie scream, one tinged with laughter, like accelerating down a drop on a roller coaster. Her sounds came in waves—

long and extended one moment, and then short little pants the next. The man grunted with each thrust. He had a dark brown mustache and bowl-cut hair. His sweat dripped on her stomach, her breasts. The woman was a brunette, her legs wrapped around his waist. Her breasts trembled. They were beautiful. She grabbed them, squeezed, and pinched her nipples.

Bon Jovi sang "Bad Medicine." His raspy voice blended with slurps, slaps, and sucks. Kevin turned up the volume and the sex got louder. Deafeningly loud. He laughed and pointed, laughed and pointed, hopping up and down on the couch like a kid waiting for his birthday cake. Mike kept repeating, "Awesome, awesome." Sampan looked at the TV and then looked away, looked at it again and looked away.

The couple went at it for another minute or two. Then the man pulled out.

I blinked and blinked again.

He was large. Larger than even my father, who I'd accidentally seen after a shower and once at the urinal in the men's room. This man had a penis I imagined superheroes possessed. Men bitten by radioactive spiders or with Adamantium skeletons or who had crashed down from Krypton. A penis with superpowers.

The man said, "Blow me," and the woman went down there and didn't blow anything. Suddenly, grunting, the man spasmed and spasmed. Something shot out of his penis that wasn't pee, but thick and white.

"What the fuck?" I said.

"Semen," Sampan whispered.

"She's licking it," Mike said.

"Gross," Kevin said, and we all agreed.

There was another sex scene that followed and we watched that for a bit before Kevin said, "There's something else." He motioned us to his parents' bedroom, which was pink and dark, the shades drawn shut. It smelled of overpowering cologne and perfume, of musk and potpourri. Kevin crouched under the bed, lifting up a frilly dust ruffle. He pulled out a shoebox and opened it.

In the box was a twelve-inch replica of a penis. It had balls. Thick veins ran along the sides. Kevin grabbed it by the sac with two fingers.

"It's sticky," Kevin said.

Mike started to chatter-gun laugh through his teeth.

"I think my dad uses this with my mom."

"Doesn't he have one of his own?" Mike said.

I wondered the same thing.

"Maybe your dad's dick is busted," said Mike.

"Shut up," Kevin said.

Mike said it again.

Kevin thrust the dildo in Mike's face. Mike leapt to his feet with a screech and ran out the door, saying broken dick, broken dick. Kevin chased him, dildo in hand.

Sampan and I were in the bedroom, sitting on Kevin's parents' bed. The blanket was a design of flowers and pink stripes. On this bed, I thought, people had sex. I wondered whether mine did too. I wondered whether my parents had a dildo under their bed. They weren't affectionate. Sometimes they held hands. Sometimes they slow danced at golf banquets. Most of the time, they kept a polite distance from one another. At school, I had learned about asexual animals, re-creation though mitosis, cells splitting and forming, a different type of miracle. My parents seemed asexual. They seemed void of passion and desire. I think I knew this even when I was younger. I remember when I was five forcing my father to kiss my mother before he left for work. I remember how she stuck out her cheek and how his scratchy face neared hers, his lips barely touching her skin. I remember how my mother cupped the side of her face, as if trying to capture the essence of his breath.

Sampan and I went back into the living room and lowered the volume on the porno.

"You have the greatest friends in the world," Sampan said.

A few minutes later, Kevin's white van pulled into the driveway. I screamed, "Parents," and immediately Kevin put the dildo back, popped the tape out of the VCR, and put it in his father's underwear drawer.

That night, we watched Hulk Hogan and Brutus "The Barber" Beefcake take down Zeus and Randy "Macho Man" Savage. From bodies rolling around in bed to bodies rolling around on the mat. We cheered, we cursed. But all of us were thinking of sex—blowing and stroking, and boobs and dicks, and when it would be our time for such marvelous things.

The Falls

My father liked the stage. He didn't mind the blinding spot-light or the blush coating his dark brown cheeks. In the last few months, he had been in the activities room at temple, working on grace and nimbleness. He'd volunteered to dance at His Majesty's birthday celebration, a day where hundreds of Thais from Illinois, Wisconsin, and Indiana gathered at the Drake Hotel ballroom to eat and drink and watch performances of *lum,* classical Thai dancing. Throughout the month of November, my father fiercely protected his hands, kept them in thin gloves and refused to wear his wedding ring for fear of a tan line. Instead of practicing his putts, he practiced dancing, bending his body to the music, arching his callused fingers. This year King Bhumibol Adulyadej turned sixty-two, and in Thailand, he was waking up to the hot sun. But here, the cold Lake Michigan wind whipped against the lighted Chicago skyline.

That night, my mother looked like the Queen of Thailand, lovely in the dress she had spent months sewing. It was the color of a good red wine, made from soft Thai silk. The shoulders were puffed up, but not like a bad prom dress, and the buttons were faux gold. My mother put on red lipstick that matched the dress, and Aunty Sue—who had to work that night—had helped put her hair into a tight beehive.

I loathed the King's birthday celebrations. The best part of the night was usually the open bar where I could order unlimited Shirley Temples. This year, I expected things to be different. Sampan had planned to come, but when Tasanee arrived without him, I quickly found a phone and dialed his number.

"Where are you?"

"I'm sick," he coughed. "I'm—"

I hung up.

Simon strutted around the Drake lobby like a rock star. He strolled over in a fitted navy blue suit and shiny black shoes.

"Did your daddy dress you?" Simon said.

I kept my back to him.

"You look like Pee-wee Herman," he said.

I moved away. He followed.

"Your mom looks nice today. Did she make that dress?"

I plucked a petal from a flower decoration.

"Where's your boyfriend?"

"Leave me alone." I turned toward him. I wanted to un-pretty Simon's prettiness—bloody his outfit, crush his nose, and knock out his teeth. My hands fisted. I bit at my lip. It wasn't Simon I was angry at. It wasn't Sampan who was sick at home, probably drowning in guilt. It was the fact that I needed him so badly to make this night bearable, the fact that I felt most uncomfortable around large groups of Thais, my anxiety building in my shoulders and neck, spreading to every inch of my body. I came to temple only for him, and he for me. Without the other, we were lost.

Simon smirked. "What?" he said.

I lifted the bridge of my glasses with my middle finger.

He rolled his eyes. "You're an idiot."

"I hate you."

Simon connected his thumbs and formed a W with his fingers, *whatever,* and then he walked away, climbed the escalator, and disappeared.

The Thai community made sure the King's celebration was the largest event of the year. Preparations started six months prior to his birthday bash, and most Thais donated their time and energy to see that the festivities went without a hitch. My family helped in whatever manner they could. My mother sold tickets for the event. Aunty Sue typed and stapled together the programs. My father and Tasanee were on a committee that met each Sunday to discuss what to have for dinner, what local Thai businesses would help sponsor the night, and when to toast the King.

With the exception of Buddha, I didn't understand such devotion to royalty. "What's the big deal?" I'd said once. To me, the King stole one of my Saturday nights in front of the television. To me, he was no more special than our newly elected president, George H. Bush, who had a last name teenage boys made jokes about.

"He is King," said my mother.

"Great man," said my father.

"Kindest heart," said Aunty Sue.

Still, the King was as distant to me as the ten cousins I had never met in Thailand, as distant as Thailand had become. I had begun to dread the question, "Where do you come from?" I stopped praying to Buddha at night, and stopped speaking Thai at home. So when asked, I gave a smartass answer. "I'm a Chicagoian."

I tried to sneak away and find a dark room. In the last few months, I kept thinking about love stories, tragic ones like *Romeo and Juliet.* I was thirteen, about nine months away from high school, and was transforming from a comic book nerd to a love-hungry romantic. I began to see love stories everywhere.

At Simmons, boys and girls were dating and breaking up daily. Mike had a girlfriend, Kelly Sullivan, a tall girl who ran on the track team. In one of the many notes they passed back and forth, he had asked her: "Who is your favorite X-Men?" Kevin said he was seeing a girl his older brother knew. He told tall tales that made Mike and me wonder about her existence. "Dude, she has the biggest titties in the world." "Dude, I got to second base." "Dude, she's a high schooler." My two buddies since first grade had girlfriends—real or imagined—and I was struggling to find mine. Perhaps it was jealousy that drove me to write at night, stories of unrequited love. At the Drake, another story began percolating in my head, one about love in the truest sense and a chemistry class and a shattered petri dish and murder.

While I mulled over some of the details of the story, Tasanee handed me a video camera. She asked me to film my father's performance. She danced opposite him. The red satin princess.

I climbed to the balcony of the ballroom, which wasn't in use, and found a spot with an unobstructed view of the dance floor. I fiddled around with the camera, aiming it here and there, zooming in and out. I zoomed in on my doctor's wife, zoomed in on her bosom and watched it heave with laughter. I zoomed in on Simon, who played with his leftover sorbet, stabbing it with a spoon. Then, through the viewfinder, I saw my mother, the two chairs on either side of her empty. She smiled, her chin in her left palm, watching and listening to the band.

A few minutes later, the lights dimmed and classical Thai music played over the speakers—the rapid clinking of bells, the soft sounds of a *Khlui,* a Thai flute. The red satin princess slowly sashayed onto the center of the dance floor, dropping flower petals from a woven basket. She did not move like a princess. Her steps were too hard, her arms waved like a tree in a violent wind. In the practices before this performance, the dance instructor had said she was to move like an elegant peacock, but she resembled a staggering pigeon. My father, however, when he entered, *was* the poor peasant boy. His hands rotated nimbly, fingers arching to the rhythms of the music. There was need and urgency in his movements, of desperation and desire. Around the dance floor, the peasant and princess weaved in and out like twining vines. They embraced, and she pulled away. Embraced, pulled away. It was a game. The princess led the peasant boy on. In the end, the princess disappeared, and the peasant boy was left alone, staggering and lost.

After the performance, I headed to the dressing room. My father removed his peasant costume and put on his suit again. He didn't say much, and I didn't tell him how he was the better dancer, how I was moved by his every step.

In the suite's living room area, Tasanee was still in costume, still in character. She asked me to film the rest of the night, whatever I wanted. She put her arms around my father's neck. I focused the camera on her face.

"Did we dance well?" she asked.

"Yeah," I said.

"Did you see how handsome your papa is in makeup?"

I closed in on her small mouth. "He looked like a girl," I said.

"So pretty." She gave my father one last squeeze and pranced away.

I put the camera down. My father smiled, his lips vivid red. "Go see mama," he said.

I didn't go to my mother. I did what Tasanee had instructed. I filmed whatever I wanted. Close-ups of cigarette butts and gum. The insides of garbage cans. Images of unfinished plates of food—mangled chicken, clumps of potatoes. I wandered the hotel, filming various objects, various people.

In an unoccupied ballroom next to the King's party, I noticed a dark figure sitting in the corner, humming. The room was dark, save a light at the other end. But I knew the shape of that head. I knew that hum, which sounded like a buzz of a fly. It was Simon. He leaned back on a chair and flipped a coin, saying heads or tails to himself. I hid behind the door and filmed him for a couple minutes. I had the urge to announce I was there, to call him a name or make an obscene gesture, to continue our feud against one another. But tonight, no matter how much I hated him, I understood his urge to escape and seek solitude in a dark room. Today, we were in the same boat, bored and alone on the King's 62nd birthday.

An hour later, my father returned to the ballroom. I headed back to the balcony. The band started playing slow songs. My father sat next to my mother, their mouths close to each other's ears. My mother must've said how wonderful he was, how he danced like a *taiwada,* an angel. She pulled a Kleenex from her purse and handed it to him. He wiped the lipstick from his lips and scrubbed at his cheeks. He went into his pocket and pulled out his ring, slipping it back on his finger. Then they rose together and walked to the crowded dance floor and found a spot in the center, surrounded by other dancing couples. I recorded the two of them dancing for a few songs. My father's hand was on her waist. My mother was laughing at the chandelier ceiling.

The next morning, Sampan called to apologize. I forgave him immediately. He told me he watched the tape.

"Why did you film a toilet flushing?" Sampan asked.

I thought about it, remembering zooming in and out of the hole, the water swirling and swirling. "I don't know," I said.

A doctor donated a peacock and peahen to the *wat* as a symbol of luck and prosperity. Over the years, the Thai community had grown, and over the years Wat Dhammaram expanded. The temple had gotten enough money to install security cameras in every corner, pave the gravel parking lot, and start building a modern banquet hall attached to the back. More Thais attended sermons on Sundays. More students were enrolled into Sunday school. We were prospering.

But as for the birds, the monks kept them in a large cage filled with perches and soft hay. The cage stood in the middle of a soccer field that was converted into a vegetable garden. The birds walked and pecked the air, their feathers folded into a long tail. When they first arrived, young children banged on the cage for them to fan open, but they ignored them, turning their crowned heads the other way like high-class socialites with big hats. After the novelty of having exotic birds died down, when no one visited them as often anymore, Sampan and I had them to ourselves. We'd enter the cage, one at a time, and sit on our toes, clucking softly. We fed them bits of lettuce and cucumber, the male snatching the vegetables from our hands and delivering them to the female standing on the highest perch like a queen. Because we asked nothing of them, did not demand in a shrill voice, they opened up to us and we remained as quiet as we could to make the moment last.

Sampan and I wondered whether they were siblings or boyfriend and girlfriend, and concluded it was the latter. They seemed to need one another beyond blood relation. I watched them with amazement, with a touch of sadness.

In April 1976, my mother, father, and Aunty Sue vacationed in Niagara Falls, Canada. I was in my mother's stomach, near the end of the second trimester. What my mother remembered most were the roar of the crashing water, the fine mist that coated her windbreaker, the rainbow that arced from the Canadian side to the U.S. and my hard kicks on her stomach. This was where I inherited my fear of heights and bridges, she believed, my phobia of looking over high precipices. My family was only two years old then, and for those two years they had moved from apartment

to apartment, struggling with low wages, with country and culture, with, perhaps, the idea of being parents whether they were
ready or not. Since their arrival, they had not been outside the
state of Illinois, let alone outside the country. Aunty Sue had suggested the trip as a celebration before their lives changed in three
months with my emergence into the world.

When my mother and aunt received the same vacation days
in early June in 1990, my mother proposed revisiting Niagara
Falls, a family vacation before a momentous change in *my* life:
high school. She had asked Tasanee whether she and Sampan
would like to come along. Ecstatic, Sampan began packing for
a month-long trip instead of four days, cramming his Nintendo and his entire video game collection, thirty comic books,
three pairs of shoes, five baseball caps, and clothes for every
occasion into two oversized duffles.

For twelve hours, the air-conditioning blasted from the minivan vents. My mother forfeited the front seat to Tasanee and sat
with Aunty Sue in the second row. The cooler, the rice maker,
and assorted foods were gathered at their feet. Sampan and I
chilled in the third row, our excitement hardly contained.

When my mother and Aunty Sue snoozed through Erie,
Pennsylvania, Tasanee fed my father grapes. Sampan had dozed
off on my shoulder some time past Cleveland. His breathing
came in quick gusts. I stayed as still as I could, so I wouldn't
wake my best friend or my mother and aunt, so my father and
Tasanee wouldn't know I was watching them. They talked in
whispers, smiled and laughed silently. She touched the back of
his hair. For a moment, I thought I had been sleeping myself
and was having one of those strange dreams that seemed to be
a continuation of what was happening in the outside world. I
had plenty of dreams like that.

It had registered that Tasanee was feeding my father grapes,
that it was her fingers meeting his lips, her fingers caressing the
back of his head. I had seen my mother feed my father food on

road trips to Wisconsin Dells or Mackinaw Island in Michigan, but it never seemed romantic. Part of me knew I was witness to something that was wrong. Part of me wanted to speak up, to wake my mother, to tell Tasanee to get her hands out of my father's mouth. All of this was negated by the fact that my best friend was drooling on my shoulder.

When we crossed the New York border, Sampan told me his dream about Melinda Stein, the girl he was infatuated with. In a yearbook photo, Melinda looked Asian with sharp squinty eyes and a dark complexion, but Sampan said she was Jewish. He thought he was in love because he sweated every time she stepped into the classroom.

"You think that's love?" he asked.

"Maybe." I looked out the window; the image of my father taking grapes from Tasanee occupied my brain.

"Have you ever been in love?"

"I think so."

"How do you know?"

"I don't."

"You know everything."

"I don't have all the answers, Sam."

It was the most truthful I had ever been with him. I wanted to take back the comment and start preaching about the nature and beauty of love. I wanted to rant about the brilliance of romantic movies like *When Harry Met Sally* or *Cutting Edge.* I wanted to be that comic strip I saw in the *Chicago Sun Times* most Sundays, the one with two naked cherub-babies with a bubble over their heads that read "Love is. . . ."

Sampan stared at the rows and rows of vineyards zooming by outside the car window. We were in wine country. New York sped by in grapes.

"I think about it all the time, though," I said. "I write about it."

"Stories?"

I nodded.

"Love stories?"

Another nod.

"Tell me one."

I told him my newest creation, one that revolved around a song and a group of teenage boys who ran away and met Iowan girls in a field of cows. The boys were beckoned by three beautiful voices—I had just read the section about the sirens in the *Odyssey*. The voices sang "Heaven" by Warrant, a long-haired rock band that was popular at the end of the eighties. I obsessed over the song day and night, recording it repeatedly on one cassette and then listening to it endlessly. As the Iowan girls sang, the boys plodded through the cow-pie field. The boys were in love, entranced by the lyrics in the song . . . *Heaven isn't too far away, closer to it everyday* . . . When they reached the Iowan girls who had high hair-sprayed hair and wore G-string bikinis, the song ended and the girls disappeared.

"They were ghosts," I said. "They were—I don't know—that feeling you get when Melinda Stein walks into the room."

"What happens to the boys?"

"They kill themselves."

Sampan tilted his head. "Why?"

"That's what I imagined brokenhearted people do."

A fine mist floated over the Falls, as if this geographical wonder created its own weather. Even the temperature, which hovered in the eighties most of the day, got cooler with each step, like a million little fans were spitting a fine spray on us.

The Falls were lit up. Red, blue, green. Because I was scared of heights, one hand grabbed my glasses and the other my hat. Sampan skipped on ahead and leaned across the guardrail. He looked as if he might tip over.

"Dude," I said, but Sampan couldn't hear me over the roar. He smiled and sighed and hung over the top bar. "Dude," I said again, "be careful." I stepped toward the Falls and then stepped back.

Sampan turned. "You can do it," he said. "Don't be scared."

I took another step back. "We're high up."

Sampan came to my side. He grabbed me under the arm. "I'll be right here," he said. "Close your eyes if you have to."

I closed them.

I felt his hand lead me to the edge. I felt the ground firmly beneath me. I gripped the brim of my hat tight, my glasses even tighter.

My fear of heights had never been about the fear of falling, but about the things I would lose. It is something I never overcame, even when I was in college and took my mother on an outing to Garden of the Gods, a nature spot with deadly cliffs and drop offs. Once, she disappeared over an edge, and I expected to see her body broken, to see her dead. When I finally made it to the edge and looked down, there she was, on another landing, laughing at my fright, laughing and saying, "I'm right here. I'm right here."

"I'm right here," Sampan said. He squeezed my arm. "On three, open your eyes."

I nodded.

"One, two, three."

I opened up. My glasses were covered in mist, but the Falls were still there, the thunderous crash of water over the boulders and rocks below, and the lights painting the white rush into a cascading rainbow.

Sampan's hand was still under my arm, and wow was all we could say. Wow, wow, wow. I leaned over, my best friend beside me, feeling safer than I had ever felt, not caring whether I'd tip over.

At the hotel, Sampan unpacked, utilizing all the drawers, separating his socks from his underwear, his pants from his shorts. Before hanging his button-downs in the closet, he used the hotel iron, making sure every crease was perfect and crisp. Each morning, he woke up at seven and showered for thirty minutes, humming indecipherable teeny-bop songs. Because he was a year older, he spent ten minutes shaving, and I watched how he slowly dragged the razor through the froth of the shaving cream. After his shower and shave, he made his bed, pulling the sheets tight, and then opened the curtains so the sun lit up the room.

I was a slob. I tossed my clothes in every direction, in every corner. I rarely showered, but coated myself in cheap cologne. In the morning, the sheets on my bed were tussled and twisted around me like a cocoon. My messiness overwhelmed Sampan. He began picking up after me, putting my clothes in neat piles, color coordinating them as he saw fit. He started making my bed. Once I told him housekeeping would see to it, but he simply said, "Yeah, I know," in the way that made me believe this was something he needed done so his day would remain bright and cheery.

We had the room to ourselves. My father was supposed to sleep with us, but because we stayed up till two in the morning playing video games, he retreated to the "mom" room a floor above and spent the rest of the vacation there.

The hotel room became our apartment. That was what we called it. A foreshadowing of the future, Sampan said, when we were older and rich, our families living together, our beautiful wives out on shopping dates, our children enrolled in the same school for the gifted. There was no doubt in our minds this would happen. This was our image of the perfect life because we couldn't imagine being without one another.

During the day, Sampan wanted to spend most of his time at the Falls. He never tired of them. After breakfast at some cheap pancake house on Clifton Hill, Sampan greeted the Falls with the same awe and enthusiasm as our first night. We did the touristy things with my mother and aunt—the *Maid of the Mist* and *Journey Behind the Falls*—but most of the time, Sampan and I found a nice place to sit and watch the descending water. He brought his sketchbook and drew pages and pages of waterfalls. I brought my notebook and began writing a new story, about two friends who lived happily ever after.

I had been drawn to the weird and fantastic since the first day I met Mike on the playground years ago, when he sat down next to me on the park bench and plopped open the *Guinness Book of World Records.* I had convinced Sampan to go to the Ripley's Believe It or Not Museum to see what crazy things existed in the world.

My father and Tasanee accompanied us. Sampan's mother had complained of headaches the entire trip. Most of the time, she sat by the Falls and fanned herself with old newspapers. That night, however, she came along and waited at the exit of the museum with my father.

Sampan and I went from oddity to oddity: wax replicas of the tallest man in world, the fattest, the man with four pupils; there was a white kitten with two heads, the Fiji Mermaid, which had the torso of a monkey and the bottom half of a fish, and a calf with six legs; there were altar bowls made from the skulls of saints, a model of the Statue of Liberty constructed entirely out of matchsticks, medieval cat armor, art created from lint, quilts weaved from human hair, and the incredible shrunken head.

Halfway through the museum, when Sampan was still marveling at ancient torture devices, I came upon the Vampires Killing Kit, which was said to have been used by travelers in Eastern Europe in the eighteenth and nineteenth centuries. The kit was comprised of an old-style gun, round silver and lead bullets, five vials of holy water, a cross, a Bible, a wooden stake, and a head of garlic.

"Check it out," I said. "Believe it or not?"

Sampan glanced over my shoulder. "Not," he said.

"Mike and I have been talking since third grade about being vampires. It would be great to live forever."

We made our way to a room that resembled an eerie cemetery. The lights were dimmed and smoke wafted from the walls. A faraway wind whispered from a hidden speaker. A fake tree branched over the graves. We stopped in front of a few tombstones with funny epitaphs.

"If you live forever," Sampan said, "you'll see too many people die."

"But you remain young. Imagine what video games will be like in a hundred years. Imagine traveling the world."

"But think about your mom dying and your dad and Mike and Kevin and me and all the others you know. Think about losing them. And then think about losing them again."

I didn't want to think about that. My mother always said that one day I would be without her. Without my father. Without Aunty Sue. This was inevitable. We are born. We live. We die. And then we do it again. I hated this talk. When I was younger, four or five, I cried at the thought of death, the thought of the absence of my family, and it would take my mother hours to calm me down, to tell me she wasn't going anywhere yet. Older, I told her to keep quiet. I didn't want to hear silly talk. I'd rather concentrate on living, I said. My mother laughed and said how American I was becoming, how Americans never worry about anything. "Thai people live with the knowledge of death always in their head," she said.

Deep down I knew vampires did not exist. But I wanted to believe. I wanted to believe that I could preserve everything and everyone I loved in this world. I wanted to believe that if I wished hard enough we would never change, a state of immortal bliss. My family would always be my family. My friends would always be my friends. I wanted to tell Sampan I'd make everyone I loved into a vampire, but I knew there were rules to being an undead, that a vampire couldn't go around making anyone part of their coven, at least that was what I had read in some novels. Vampires yearned for exactly what Sampan was trying to explain. The beauty of mortality. To be alive. To have a beginning and to have an end.

I looked away and read an epitaph: "Here lies Lester Moore. Four slugs from a .44. No Less. No More."

I didn't want to be no more. I didn't want to be without Sampan. "I'd make you a vampire," I said.

"Thanks," he said and smiled in a way that made me feel young, made me realize the year difference in our ages was as large as the Falls.

We went through the museum quickly and met up with my father and Tasanee. As we made our way back to the hotel, to anybody that passed, we appeared to be a typical Asian family— a mother and father, two chubby brothers straggling behind. No one would ever know there were two other women, waiting at the hotel, preparing our dinner, two women who made sure we were fed on our vacation, who kept maps and directions close at hand. On Clifton Hill that summer night we fit the cultural expectations of the ideal family—happy and content, traveling close and in stride.

We arrived in Oak Lawn in the evening via Detroit's Canadian border. My mother had instructed my father to drop Sampan and Tasanee off and come directly home. He agreed, and we made the hour trek to Skokie, a predominately Jewish suburb. Sampan lived in a gritty neighborhood, down the street from a 7–11 and Dempster Avenue. His house was no larger than mine, a bi-level of clay-colored bricks. I had been to Sampan's often in the summer, after golf tournaments, and considered it my own home.

We didn't follow my mother's instruction. It was three in the morning when my father and I arrived home. My mother sat on the steps to the upstairs, her hair in curlers, a blue sweater wrapped around her shoulders. Her mouth was tight, her cheeks sagging.

"Go sleep," she told me sharply.

I trudged upstairs and collapsed onto my bed. I figured my father was in trouble for disobeying my mother, but it was my summer break, the last one before I entered high school. My father had only done what I wanted, had only done the thing that brought me the most happiness. He wanted the best of everything for me, always had.

Through my bedroom door, I could hear them. My mother's harsh whispers were like hisses. My father's voice was soft and sleepy and pleading. I couldn't hear what they said. I didn't know how long it lasted. I didn't care.

My mind had reverted back to Canada. I closed my eyes and began to dream about plummeting down the Falls in a barrel, like Annie Taylor, like Bobby Leach, like Charles G. Stephens, plummeting and plummeting, crashing into the pool of water, resurfacing like a bobber on a fishing line, bouncing up and down, up and down, unscathed.

The next day, I woke up to an unsettling quiet. My mother sat at her sewing machine. Her hair was uncombed and puffy, her eyes heavy with dark circles. She stared out the bay window, body hunched over, and her arms resting on her thighs. Aunty Sue cooked in the kitchen, the TV on low. The sound of daytime television whispered through the house. My father stayed upstairs for most of the afternoon until he had to leave for work. Throughout the day, no one said a word.

The next two weeks were much the same. I told Sampan about it on the phone. He said his mother was acting weird, too, and his cat, Tubby, was meowing at the water heater for no reason. "Maybe it has something to do with the moon," he said.

Perhaps, but a strangeness floated over my days. My mother and aunt talked in whispers, and when I entered the room, they'd abruptly stop. Aunty Sue showered me with gifts and food, more than the usual. My mother hugged and touched me often and without reasons why, without her usual playfulness. Most of the time, her affections were followed by a tug at my earlobes or a pinch on the underside of my arm, but now they were just hugs that were long and tight. In the weeks after our vacation, it seemed that my mother's energy was sapped. She walked as if she were tied to a weighted ball, and sighed hard as if to expel the bad from her body. And my father. He stopped calling in the evening to check up on me. What was most alarming was he wasn't coming home from work on time. For my entire life, I had timed it out. I listened for his car coasting up the driveway, for the garage door to rattle open, for the click of the backdoor lock. I knew my father would arrive between 11:27 and 11:32, and if he stopped to buy chicken wings, 11:45. Lately, however, he didn't arrive till one or two in the morning. I asked him where he went. He told me he was telling fortunes.

Every birthday, my mother would make me go to temple to bring monks their morning meal and receive my birthday blessing. Aunty Sue rose at four, the sky still dark, and began cooking. She roasted two chickens, made a green curry stew with chunks of beef, stir-fried chicken and broccoli, deep fried thin slices of eggplant, and cooked two steaming tubs of jasmine rice. My mother put crisp twenty-dollar bills into individual envelopes and drove to the grocery store for toilet paper, Irish Spring soap, toothpaste and toothbrushes, and small boxes of laundry detergent. These were our offerings to the monks, who lived off the generosity of their worshipers.

In the past, my mother and aunt invited their friends, who would come with dishes of their own. But this time she wanted a quiet birthday, family only. When we pulled into the parking lot I was surprised to see Sampan's golden Cadillac. My mother mumbled something under her breath, but I didn't hear her. I didn't care. I rushed in and found Sampan in the dining room, wiping down tables.

"Happy birthday," he said. "Listen, there's a big surprise in store for you."

"A present?"

"This is better."

"Better than a present?"

Aunty Sue announced over the intercom that the meal was ready. Monks began filing into the kitchen. Eight of them sat at two tables, while the ninth one sat by himself. That monk kept his head down so I couldn't see his face.

I delivered the plates of food for blessings. I walked with my head hung low and presented each dish in both hands. I then backed away and put my hands together and bowed my head. When it was time to present the lone monk his food, I almost burst into laughter. The monk was not a monk at all. He was a *nane,* a young novice, ordained for a brief time to bring good karma to the family. He was Simon.

Bald Simon. Shaved eyebrows Simon.

"Oh my god," I said.

My mother nudged me along. "*Tawai,*" she said. I presented the food as she instructed, my lips twitching.

"*Wai,*" said my mother. Pay your respects.

I jerked my hands up and bowed my head.

Simon narrowed his eyes.

I mouthed *baldy.* He secretly flicked me off. Then his hand retreated back into his robes.

As the monks ate, I checked whether anyone needed anything else.

"I want a Coke," Simon said.

I filled a Styrofoam cup with Coke and offered it to him the way I was supposed to.

"This cup is too small. I want a larger glass."

"Screw you," I said.

"Now."

Sampan came up beside me and filled a tall glass.

"There's not enough carbonation," Simon said.

The Chaoawad, who sat at the head of the table nearest us, had been watching the whole time. He told Simon to shut up and eat.

Throughout the meal, my mother did not talk to Tasanee, did not acknowledge her presence. She treated Sampan in the same manner, walking briskly past him, ignoring his greeting. When he asked me what was wrong, I told him she always stressed out on my birthday. Each year I grew older, she often said to me, was one more year toward losing me. But today, she acted as if the world had wronged her.

After the meal, my aunt, Sampan, and Tasanee stayed behind to clean up the kitchen and dining room.

The monks walked to the main temple. My mother and I followed. My father had been there the whole time, sitting in front of the golden statue of Buddha, praying. I didn't know when he arrived, but was glad he was there. He kissed my forehead, and I wiped the smudge of his lips away. I sat between my parents, and we kowtowed to the statue of Buddha three times, and kowtowed to the monks who had found their spots on the raised platform. The Chaoawad opened an ornate copper bowl filled with holy water and lit a yellow candle above it. The wax dripped into the bowl. The water hissed.

This had become my birthday ritual, so when the Chaoawad nodded to me, I knew what to do. I walked on my knees toward the statue of Buddha and lit two candles and three incenses that were stuck in a bowl of sand. I began to pray, asking the

Chaoawad in *Pali* for *sila,* instruction in the Five Precepts and Triple Gem.

"*Mayam bhante visum visum rakkhanatthaya, tisaranena saha pancasilani yacama.*"

I repeated the prayer three times.

After I completed it, the Chaoawad launched into another invocation, his voice deep and filled with bass. The other monks followed his lead, their chants intertwining. When one voice dropped out to take a breath, another rose to fill the void. It was symphonic. I never understood what the prayers meant, but I closed my eyes and imagined the image of Buddha like my mother had told me throughout my life. I sat on my toes, my heels under my behind. I took a peek at my mother and father whose lips were in tune with the prayer. I snuck a look at Simon who sat above me, sneering. He stuck out his tongue, and I stuck out mine.

Near the end of the prayer, the Chaoawad dipped what looked like the whiskers of a witch's broom into the copper pot and sprinkled the water on me, his voice never skipping a beat. The water hit off the top of my head, my neck and back. It soaked into my skin. The whiskers rattled. He kept doing it, showering my parents and me with blessings. By the end, I was wet, but felt cleansed, felt that fourteen would be a new and better year in my life.

When the ceremony ended, my mother got up quickly, not saying a word to my father, who turned to Buddha again and began to pray. I left to find Sampan, who waited outside for me on a picnic table, under the shade of an oak.

"I've never been to one of these," Sampan said.

"It gets boring."

"Still, it's one day, right?"

"Yep."

"You feel good, right?"

"Yep."

"And it's totally worth it to see Simon bald, right?"

"Totally."

Simon came outside, his flip-flops slapping his heels, and wandered over to the fence that separated the temple from Nottingham Park. He carried a watering bucket with him and began watering some of the pansies in a flowerbed. He ignored us. We ignored him.

On the other side of the fence were a couple of boys, playing basketball. They wore dirty jeans and ripped black T-shirts. They stopped shooting as Simon watered the flowers. They whispered to each other, their hands over their mouths. One of them—the bigger of the two—whipped the ball at the fence. Simon didn't flinch, didn't stop what he was doing.

"Hey, monk," the big boy said. "Nice robes."

Simon kept watering.

"Hey, I'm talking to you."

Simon adjusted his robes and moved to another flower. To him, these boys were background noise. They were inanimate like the swing, the teeter-totter, the monkey bars.

"I bet if he took off those robes there'd be a small weenie," the smaller boy said.

The big boy laughed and made his pinky go up and down. "Hey, monk, are you dumb or something?"

The big boy picked up a pebble and tossed it over the ten-foot fence. It landed near Simon's feet. Simon kept watering. The boy picked up another pebble and tossed it over. And another. One finally hit Simon on the top of his bald head. He dropped the water bucket and turned toward the fence.

"What?" said the big boy.

Simon's back heaved up and down.

"I'll come over there and waste you."

His friend laughed hard and loud. "I think he's gonna cry," he said. "I think the little monk boy is going to cry."

Simon didn't move.

"Don't look at us that way," said the big boy. He put his feet in the chain link and started to climb. His friend jumped up and down, yelling, "Kick his ass. Kick that monk's ass."

I couldn't stand it anymore. I was fourteen and wanted to prove it. I rose and took large strides toward the fence, Sampan jogging behind. My adrenaline carried me to Simon's sides in seconds.

"You want some of this, too?" said the boy on the fence. He was nearing the top.

"When you get down here, I will kick your fuckin' teeth in," I said.

The boy kept climbing. He talked all the way up. "Pussies. I'll tear you apart."

"Stop talking." I kicked the fence. I punched it as hard as I could. I screamed like a mad man. "Get over here." I bounced from side to side. The skinny boy on the ground stopped laughing. The boy on the fence turned red.

"Got nothing to say now?" I said. "You scared?"

Sampan made a chicken noise.

"Fuck you," said the skinny boy.

"Fuck you," said the big boy. As he swung his leg over, I grabbed a pebble and whipped it at his head. When he ducked, his pants got caught on a sharp point of the fence. The rip resounded throughout the park.

Simon fell to his knees laughing. He laughed so hard he couldn't breathe. Sampan was laughing too, pointing at the six-inch hole in the crotch of the boy's jeans.

"Hey, tighty whitey," I said.

"Fuck you," said the boy. "Fuck you." He quickly swung his leg back to the other side of the fence and climbed down, covering his behind. "Next time I see any of you I'll waste you," the boy said.

"Next time, change your underwear," I said.

They ran off into the neighborhood, disappearing around a bend.

"Holy shit," Simon said, getting off the ground.

"Holy shit," Sampan said.

I turned to leave. My body surged with energy.

"Wait," Simon said.

I stopped.

"Thanks."

"Whatever," I said.

"You're bleeding," said Simon.

I looked at my right hand. The chain link had cut between some of my knuckles.

"Bring it here," Simon said.

"Why?"

"Just do it."

Simon picked up the watering bucket and tipped it onto my wound

"It's holy water," he said. "The temple's water is holy water."

The three of us spent the rest of the afternoon sitting in the temple's main office, playing video games. Simon was an animated player, jumping up and down, swearing up a storm when his character died. Sampan and I said *nanes* shouldn't speak like that, and Simon said, "Fuck it."

Simon was never Simon anymore, but just another Thai kid who was as lonely and lost as many of us were. A week later, he was no longer a *nane*, but he never said anything bad to me again. He never said anything, except for a nod. Eight years later, I saw him at a Thai grocery store. He was a businessman in imports and exports and thrilled to see me, speaking of our past as if we had been the best of friends. "Good times," he kept saying. "Good times."

Bad Son

Kevin and I watched porn. It was all we did at his house because his parents worked nine to five, because Kevin insisted porn had to be on at all times, because each week his father had a new video with new girls. Sometimes the girls were black, Asian, or Latino, and sometimes the guy went in another hole and Kevin said, "Isn't that where they pooped?" and I said, "I think so," and he said, "Doesn't that hurt?" and I said, "How would I know?" We did other things like read or talk about the hottest new car or video game or imagine our futures as people of importance, and the porn was on as background like elevator music in department stores.

The truth was we didn't need to keep watching, but the porn was like a dark mischievous secret. Anything bad, no matter how redundant, was good.

"You want the phone yet?" Kevin said, flipping through *Road & Track*.

I checked my watch. "Ten more minutes."

In the month after my birthday, I'd gone to Kevin's to hide from the hot sun, hide from the buzzing gnats and flies that swarmed around my perspiration, hide from my mother. Around three, I used Kevin's phone to call Sampan. It was the only time we had to talk.

Whenever I called Sampan from home, I'd hear a click of my mother picking up upstairs and the sound of the receiver brushing against her cheek. She would tell me to get off in a strained and clipped voice, a voice that suggested there was more she wanted to say. She then would hang up, and I would tell Sampan how much of a bitch she was and Sampan told me not to say that and we'd try to talk later. But every time we tried, she'd do it again.

There was something wrong. I couldn't name it, but I felt it. I heard it. I knew it involved me. My mother and father argued often, their voices hushed but urgent. If I came down the stairs, they would pretend nothing was happening. My mother would look out the nearest window and my father turned on the TV.

"It's time," Kevin said.

I took the phone and dialed the number. Sampan picked up on the first ring. Kevin put the phone on speaker and raised the volume of the TV.

"Porn again?" Sampan said.

"Yeah," Kevin said, "Why not?"

We devised a plan: I would tell my mother I was sleeping over at Kevin's. Kevin's father would take us to Sampan's because my father worked, and the next morning, my father would bring us home. When Friday rolled around, Kevin called and said he couldn't go. It was his stupid brother's birthday. I quickly called Sampan while my mother hung laundry outside. As a last ditch effort, he suggested asking Aunty Sue.

My aunt read a Thai magazine upstairs in her bedroom. Her sight was going, so she used a small magnifying glass over the words.

"*Pa*," I said. I leaned in the doorway.

She looked up, but forgot to put the magnifying glass down. For a second, she had one enlarged eye.

"Sampan wanted to know if I could sleep over. Can you take me?"

Aunty Sue, who stayed out of all arguments, who always remained neutral, shook her head. "Ask mama," she said.

Downstairs, my mother was coming in with an empty laundry basket. I met her in the family room, my hands on my hips. "Can I sleep at Sampan's?"

"No," she said.

"Why?"

"Don't ask why."

"Why?" I said.

"You deaf?"

"Why are you being a bitch?"

My mother's face grew bright. It was the first time I called her a bitch, and I did not regret it. Not then. Usually, I swore liberally around my parents. I said the word "shit" and "fuck" like it was nobody's business. They didn't mind, laughed when I used it; as long as it was not directed at them, such words were permissible. The word *bitch,* however, was the first cuss word my mother learned. She had been called one by an irate patient and rude doctor. She had been called one by the backyard neighbor's boy, who was three and didn't know what it meant. *Bitch* was not a word she fully understood, but she knew it was bad and it was mean and it was something she did not want to be.

My mother's voice cracked. I was a bad son, she kept saying. I didn't love her. I loved a friend more. Bad Thai boy.

"You're crazy," I said. "*Bah!*"

My mother slapped me.

I was six foot tall. I towered over her, outweighing her by over fifty pounds. I moved my hand to swing back, but stopped short, an inch from her cheek. My breaths came quick, my body in a tight knot. My face stung. And this I remembered feeling:

overwhelming fury. In the comic books I used to read there were moments when even the best of superheroes couldn't contain their anger, when they were pushed too far, and it was these moments that they were not immune, no matter what power, to the vulnerabilities of being human that reduced them to the scariest parts of themselves. I raged. I punched the walls of the house until my fist exploded through the drywall. I kicked the couch over. I whipped the cushions into the golf trophies on the Japanese table. They crashed like bowling pins. "What is your problem?" I slammed my shoulder into the La-Z-Boy like a tackling dummy. "What is your fuckin' problem?"

My mother took a step back, but she didn't let up. Her voice roared over mine. She jabbed her finger at the angry air between us. Bad son, bad son. You love your father more, that bastard, who is sleeping with that woman. Your friend's mother.

I grabbed the closest thing in reach, a red golf ball I used to practice my putting. There were several around me. I whipped one at my mother. She covered her head. The ball collided with the front door. I had gone too far. I couldn't stop my arm from flinging another golf ball at the front bay window. The ball hit the curtain, which softened the impact, and dropped to the ground.

Before I could do anything else, Aunty Sue dashed down the stairs. She yanked my hair, her nails digging into my scalp, an electrical cord from a radio in her hand. She whipped at my legs and arms and body. "*Bab gum*," she screamed. Sinner. She pushed me onto the floor, a woman even smaller than my mother. She struck every part of my body. I didn't feel the cord. I didn't feel anything but the heaviness that was strangling my heart, the heaviness that was stealing my breath. I covered my head. The cord came down and down and down.

My aunt was crying.

My mother had run upstairs.

I curled up on the carpet.

I felt my aunt's body pressed over me. She gathered me up in her arms. I let her take me, let her push my head into her chest. I couldn't do that to my mother, she said, I couldn't do that again, not ever, no matter what she had done, I couldn't do that. She whispered in a broken voice, I'm sorry, I'm sorry.

I listened for her steps down the stairs, and for the back door to open and close, and for the station wagon to make it out of the driveway. When I was positive my mother and aunt had left for work, I moved downstairs. There were two fist-sized holes in the wall, but the rest of the house had been picked up and cleaned. I shook my head and knew this is what my mother thought Americans would do. They would rage and try to hurt her. And now her son, an American, had lost control.

I went straight for the refrigerator. I took out the Tupperware of my aunt's chicken and ate, shoving a drumstick into my mouth, tearing away chunks of it and devouring the sticky rice that was cold and hard. I ate for two straight hours. When I finished off the chicken, I cooked ramen noodles. When I finished the noodles, I fried up some eggs. I ate until midnight, my belly hard with food.

I picked up the phone and called Sampan. Tasanee answered and I hung up. I called again. She answered. I hung up. I called one more time. When she picked up, I transformed my voice and asked for Sampan. I told her my name was Pierce. I spoke with a nasally whine.

Sampan would know it was me. Pierce Tan was my pseudonym, the author of tragic love stories. Tan because Amy Tan was the only Asian writer I knew and Pierce because my stories were meant to pierce your soul.

"Hey," he said. "You kinda freaked out my mom."

"Sorry," I said.

"What are you doing?"

"I just ate a shitload of food."

"Was it good?"

I was drunk from my eating high. My eyelids were barely open.

"Are you OK?"

"Does my father come over to your house at night?"

Sampan didn't speak.

"Does he?"

"Yeah."

"For how long now?"

"For a while."

"Is he there now?"

"Yeah."

"What is he doing?"

"Talking with my mom."

"Why does he go there?"

"I don't know," he said. "My mom sometimes tells him to go home."

"He should."

More silence.

"Does he sleep there?" I asked.

"Yeah."

"Where?"

"On the couch."

"Are you telling me the truth?"

"Yes."

"He should come home. Your mom shouldn't let him in the house. He has a home. He should be here. Right now. He should be here with me." I burped, but it became more. I darted to the bathroom, the cordless phone in my hand.

"Are you OK?" Sampan's voice was faint. I hung over the toilet. When I was done, I grabbed the phone.

"Does it sound like I'm OK, Sam?"

"No."

"What are they doing now?"

"Still talking," he said. "Do you want to talk to him?"

"No."

"Are you mad at me?"

Sampan was about to cry. I heard it in his voice.

"No," I said.

I batted around everything in my head, replaying the day, the swings of extreme emotion. I rubbed at a welt on my arm. There were other welts on my legs that hurt. It all began to sting.

In Thai the word for love is *ruk*. When I was eight, I used to hear it as "lock," as in the princess *locked* away in the tower, or I *locked* my keys in the car, or the thief was *locked* away for years. I locked myself in my room and in my head. When Mike and Kevin called, I didn't answer. When they came over, I told them I was sick. Each night when my mother and aunt were at work, I ate to the point of throwing up. Binge eating was a mix of pleasure and pain, an extreme indulgence that went beyond the extended limits of the body. Two bags of Doritos, four Twinkies, and four packs of noodles took my mind off my situation at home, if only for a couple of hours.

My calls to Sampan were less frequent. Our conversations began to fill with silences, as if both us knew what we really needed to talk about, but neither of us wanted to be the first to bring it up. We no longer saw each other at temple because I no longer went. Instead, my father would go and bring back letters and drawings Sampan had sent with him. One drawing was of Spiderman webbing the word *Hello*.

At home, my mother and I continued to argue about Sampan. I pleaded with her. I told her I needed him. She begged me to see how our friendship was ruining the family. During other arguments, she employed different tactics, filled with irrationality. A boy born from evil, she kept saying, would end up just as evil. It was in the blood. She said Buddha would tell me to choose her. Sampan was the wrong path. Every few days, another argument, and each time I told her no. Not in her dreams. I would never abandon Sampan's friendship.

The truth was, at the end of each day, I thought about everything she said. Her arguments nibbled at the part of my brain that was denying my father's infidelity, denying the whole situation. My imagination carried me to places I didn't want to go. I envisioned my father and Tasanee romantically involved, kissing and holding hands in front of Buckingham Fountain. I remembered how she fed him grapes on the way to Niagara Falls. I imagined Sampan with my father, the two of them playing golf at Pebble Beach, something I dreamt of doing my entire life. I tortured myself with the Perhaps game. Perhaps Sampan wanted my father for himself, since he didn't have a father of his own. Perhaps he was evil, the spawn of Medusa, the apple not falling far from the tree. Then again, perhaps he was as confused and twisted inside as I was, not knowing what do or who to believe, having so much energy that all he wanted to do was hit something. I shook away the thoughts. I reminded myself that I loved my friend. I repeated it.

It wasn't just my mother's arguments, however, that made me sleepless and hungry. It was also her. Her sadness. Her broken heart. My mother did nothing but sew, sitting in front of the bay window. From the time she returned home from work to the time she went upstairs to sleep, my mother didn't leave her spot at the sewing machine. Her hair was in disarray, tangled and misshapen. She began to lose the hair on the top of her head. She appeared as if she hadn't slept, wearing the same orange pajamas for three weeks. Her eyes were rimmed with wetness, but I never saw her cry. I wondered what was happening to her heart. Where was her mind when she sewed her nurse's uniforms or Thai dresses? Where was she when her hand guided the fabric through the jagging needle?

Downstairs, my mother was screaming at my father. She said my father was a whore who slept with a whore who whored herself with another man to make a whore son.

I sneaked out of my room and crouched next to Aunty Sue's bedroom door. It was shut and the volume on her TV was high. She was watching a Thai soap opera and someone on the TV was crying dramatically. I sat in a shadow, hidden in the dark of the hallway, and watched my mother spit and point. Her finger was so straight it bent backward. Her voice was hoarse. She wanted to walk away, but always turned to say one more thing.

"You are a terrible father," she said in Thai. She turned, took two steps, but then whirled back. "Terrible!"

My father stared at the golf trophies, at a flickering lightbulb above the dining room table, at a picture of me dressed as a vagabond for Halloween.

"*Jai dum!*" She turned away and then turned back. "Heartless!"

My father wanted to say something. His chest rose. His mouth opened slightly. But he swallowed whatever was stuck in his throat. I wondered about the possibilities: Yes, I'm sorry. I won't do it again. Or, You yell too much. Or, You are wrong. I never slept with her.

Speak, I mentally urged. Tell us the truth. His silence infuriated me. His face sagged. His body sagged. It was as if all the bones that kept him up liquefied.

My mother thundered into the kitchen. I heard a drawer slide open, a clang of silver. When she came back into sight, she gripped a metal fireplace lighter in her hand, one that was over a foot long.

"*I bah,*" she said. "You hurt us. I will hurt you." She hit him.

She hit him on his arms. He didn't flinch, didn't move off the couch. The lighter was bending in half, bending into a ninety-degree angle.

I ran downstairs. Ran out of the house. Ran in my sleeping wear—a thin T-shirt and cutoff sweats. Ran as fast as my legs could carry me. Down McVicker. Right on 93rd. I turned left on Lynwood and passed the high school tennis courts and Mike's house. He was taking out the garbage.

"Hey," he called after me.

I didn't turn back.

"What are you doing?" He caught up and jogged alongside.

"Running," I said.

"I know," he said. "You're not wearing shoes."

I didn't respond.

"Why are you running without shoes?"

"Because my parents hate each other."

Mike knew about divorce, but he didn't seem affected by it. Never once did he complain. Never once did he say he was mad. I saw Mike almost every day for eight years and the only time he spoke about his parents split-up was when he told me to call him at his mother's instead of his father's.

Mike kept in stride with me. We ran for another block, not saying a word. It was comfortable to have him near.

I stopped. My lungs burned. My feet hurt.

"That sucks," Mike finally said.

We stood on the sidewalk houses away from his. It was dark under the trees of the drive. I could barely make out Mike's features.

"I gotta go," he said.

I nodded.

Mike headed back, as my father's minivan rounded the corner.

I started walking.

He honked.

I ignored him.

"Get in," he said.

"Leave me alone."

"Get in." His voice was firm and loud.

I stopped.

"Please," he said.

Lynwood ended in a block. If I took a left I could go to Kevin's. If I took a right I'd hit Southwest Highway, where I could hop on a bus and go . . . *where?*

"Please," he said again.

My father's brown arm hung outside the car, and his head leaned out the window. He sighed. In the last few weeks, this was more than we'd said to each other.

"Why don't you fight back?" I said.

"Please."

"You sit there and let her hit you."

"Please."

I was cold. My feet were sore and cut. I got into the minivan. I sat on the right side of the seat, trying to distance myself from my father. I stared out the window. My hand cradled my head, which pounded. My father turned on the radio and on came the Carpenters.

"You are suffering," he said. His voice caught me by surprise. It wasn't a voice I expected, not one from a person who got yelled at, not one who got hit with a foot-long metal lighter.

I leaned my head on the car window and felt the cool of the glass. We cruised down Cicero, the opposite direction from home. Despite all the anger that bubbled inside of me, I was with my father, alone, for the first times in weeks, and although there were so many unsaid things, I didn't want to leave the minivan.

"Where are we going?" I asked.

"Sampan's."

"Don't you think we need to go home?"

My father kept on the path toward the Dan Ryan Expressway, where the cars zoomed by us and the Chicago skyline sparkled in the distance. This was wrong, I wanted to tell him. We should be with my mother, who was probably waiting for me, wondering whether I would make it home tonight. I saw her at the sewing machine. I saw her follow every headlight that passed in front of the house, hoping one would turn up the driveway.

"We should go home," I whispered, more to myself than to him.

"Sampan sad," my father said.

"About what."

"Everything."

When we arrived, I headed to the basement, Sampan's room, passing Tasanee without proper greeting. No lights were on save for the glow from the television. Sampan stood in the corner of the basement, his body shaking. He sniffled and wiped his nose with the back of his hand. He knew I was there, but didn't turn around.

I sat on the sofa, which made my skin itchy, and watched him for a minute before I spoke up, before I officially announced my presence.

"Why are you crying?"

"Your mom hates me."

I didn't say anything. He cried harder.

"You hate me," he said.

I didn't say anything, so he turned. Everything about his face was red and wet and sloppy. Snot clung to a nostril. It moved when he breathed.

I felt a strange vindictive power over Sampan. I wanted him to suffer.

"Wipe your face," I said. "There's a booger hanging out your nose."

"You hate me," he said again.

He walked closer to me. I shifted my gaze to the TV. It looked new.

"New TV?"

Sampan wiped at his eyes.

"Did my dad buy it for you? Is he your daddy now?"

Sampan's mouth popped open. He ran to the bathroom and slammed the door. I reached for the remote and changed the channel. I stopped on MTV. A guy in long matted hair screamed into a mic and kept sticking out his long tongue. I nodded to the music. The rhythm of it quickened my heart. I wanted to break things.

I spilled out my remaining anger into a new story about a family destroyed by a prostitute who happened to be the main character's best friend's mother. There were no winners here. The first line: "It was a downward spiral into the darkest and deepest depths of hell." I didn't hold back. I wrote for three straight nights, wrote with vigor and passion, adjectives begetting adjectives, adverbs piled upon adverbs. Buckets of blood and vilifying violence and dastardly deaths. Everyone met tragic ends, except for the hero: the best friend's mother was hit by a truck, her body mangled to the point it was unidentifiable; the father died from castration; the mother lived the rest of her days in an asylum because she castrated the father; and the best friend, guilty by association, was murdered by the son with wooden skee balls at Chuck E. Cheese.

The son survived. He met a pretty brunette and lived happily ever after.

On Labor Day, Mike and Kevin planned to spend the night at my house one last time before the summer ended and high school started. Kevin was in charge of the movies, a porn he borrowed from his father's underwear drawer. Mike took care of the Mountain Dew and barbeque chips. I provided video games and pizza.

Before Mike and Kevin's arrival, my mother came downstairs, a blue sweater draped over her shoulders. Her face drooped. She had recently lost a lot of her teeth and had special dentures made. She didn't wear them.

I was playing *Karnov,* on the last stage of the game. My Russian hero was fighting a dragon with three heads. I pressed the buttons of the game harder, feeling my mother's stare on the side of my face. Our arguments had lessened since I ran out of the house without my shoes. Both of us had exhausted ourselves and wanted to live cordially with one another, even in silence. That evening, however, she looked like she had something on her mind.

"*Mae hen,*" she said. I saw him. "With eyes."

Karnov threw fireballs in threes at the dragon.

"Please listen," she said. "Aunty and me following him to her house. He say he go to work, but today Labor Day. No work on Labor Day. He there. I seeing car."

My Russian hero dodged the lunging dragon. I had timed my attacks. The dragon swayed like a cobra in a basket for three seconds, then struck. This was its pattern. I jumped over one of its heads and fireballed the other two.

"He wanting to be Sampan dad now," she said.

Fireball. Fireball. Fireball.

"Please," she said. "No more Sampan."

The dragon bit my Russian hero.

"Understanding?"

The dragon bit again. Bit twice in one move. Karnov died. He fell to the ground, his bare belly to the sky.

My mother continued to stare at the side of my face.

"No more Sampan," I said, my eyes still on the game. "Promise."

My mother smiled without teeth, her gums pink. She pulled at my earlobes. She played with my hair. I let her. "*Dek dee,*" she said. Good son.

Mike and Kevin arrived later in the evening, and we did the usual—played video games, watched a movie and chilled. In the last year, whenever the sleepover was at my house, we made it a ritual to sneak out at two in the morning, cutting through Jack's flower garden where a Jesus statue always stared accusingly at us to go to the high school bleachers across the street. There, we'd sit overlooking the football field, the sprinklers chatting over the lush grass.

Often, we talked about crushes and sexual urges, and sometimes our conversations drifted into deep philosophical matters.

"Could you imagine a world made up of comic book characters?" Mike said. He wore a thin black T-shirt. Mike believed in dressing in stealth during our late night breakouts.

"I'd be Metal Man," Kevin said. "Bullets bouncing off my skin." He made rapid pinging sounds.

"No," I said, "Divot Chest because of that large indentation in your chest."

"Shut up." Kevin put his hand over his divot.

Mike laughed so hard he snorted.

Next week, we would be freshmen boys, lowest on the totem pole. We heard rumors of what the upperclassmen would do to us: shove us in lockers, whip pennies at us, knock our books out of our arms, and give us wedgies. Mike and Kevin were scared. They were afraid of the changes. For me, so much had already happened in the course of a few months, I felt like high school would be another day.

For so long, I had struggled to find my place in school, from the very first day I stepped into Harnew Elementary when I folded my hands and bowed my head, when I could barely speak English. Eight years later, school was a welcomed comfort, the place I felt I belonged, and it was at home, at temple, that I felt adrift, alien. I thought about what my mother had said earlier, how she followed my father to Sampan's and found his car, and I was surprised by my acceptance of it, scared by how easily it rolled out of my thoughts. Our lives were made of a series of choices, and for my family, immigrants in a country not their own, we made plenty of wrong ones, choices that were made by our hearts, our anger, our regret, that led us further astray. I clung to the hope that we could always get back. No matter how far we went, we would find our way again.

I dug deep into my pockets. I stared across the football field. Shadows of the goal posts played across the beige exterior of the high school. "My dad's sleeping with another woman."

"That sucks," Kevin said. "Do you know who?"

"It doesn't fuckin' matter," Mike said.

Kevin leaned back. "You're right."

Mike put a hand on my shoulder, his touch so unexpected I flinched. "Fuck it," he said and squeezed.

It was sage advice, so simple it was Buddhist.

"Fuck it," I said.

"Fuck it," Kevin said.

We erupted into laughter, echoing off the building, echoing throughout the neighborhood. I hadn't laughed in over a month and now I couldn't stop. Mike had to shush me, afraid we'd get caught by the cops.

He tilted his head up and looked at the stars. "What do you think, Kev, about a planet of chicks?"

"With big knockers," Kevin said. We went on describing the world of our dreams.

This was the last summer for the three of us. When high school started, only Mike and I traveled in the same circle. Kevin dropped out after a couple of months. He got a girl pregnant two years later and became a father, struggling to keep a job as a mechanic at random garages, but insisting on buying extravagant cars. Mike and I continued our friendship through high school and became college roommates before Mike transformed into an online vampire who Rollerbladed through the dark southern Illinois woods at midnight.

That night, though, we did not foresee what was to happen to us. Because, sometimes, it wasn't possible to know where a path would lead. Sometimes we walk blindly. We knew only about the moment. We knew only that if there were a world of chicks, we would be the only men on that planet, and we fantasized about that life for an hour more, leaning against the bleachers, looking up toward the sky.

As we made our way back, I screamed cops because I thought I saw a police car turning toward us. We ducked behind the Jesus statue in my neighbor's garden, crouching behind his white robes. When the car passed, it wasn't the police at all but a plain white Buick Regal. All at once, we whooped out of our hiding places and into the street, our middle fingers raised high in the air. "Fuck you," we screamed, but the car had turned down 95th, far from the sight of our rebellious fingers.

If divorce meant we were American, then we were American. My parents stayed together for another two years. I wanted them apart. It would have made them happy, free from the weight of each other. Most days, my father lived at Sampan's house. My mother's friends called and gossiped and gave infidelity sightings: *He was in Chinatown with her, holding hands. He was at temple, flirting. That bastard, that poor excuse for a Thai man.* My mother accepted their calls and thanked them for the gossip. She had already pulled herself away from the marriage. It was the day, I believe, I told her I would stop seeing Sampan.

Every Christmas, Sampan sent me a card updating me with his life. He had gotten into the University of Michigan. He had a girlfriend. He was in love. He asked whether I still wrote stories. How was golf? He said my father was proud of me and spoke of me often. I never wrote back, but felt happy to know Sampan was moving on, happy to know he was happy.

When I was sixteen, Aunty Sue flew to Thailand. Her brother had passed away, and during the flight, her older sister died unexpectedly. During the time my aunt was away, my father moved out.

I remember watching Jay Leno on late night TV when my father walked through the door and said, "Your aunt putting curse on me in Thailand. Must go."

I didn't question the absurdity of the comment. "I'll help you pack," I said.

My father took very little with him: a picture of me and my mother, some clothes, his golf clubs and his golf trophy, and the main Buddha of the house. With everything packed, he stood by the front door.

"Where are you going?" I asked. I already knew the answer.

"Cannot tell."

"Can you give me a phone number?"

He shook his head.

"How will I stay in touch?"

He said he would call. He said he needed time. He stepped outside without saying good-bye. I followed him, rubbing my hands against my bare arms. It was January, a few weeks after the 1993 New Year, and snow drifted to the ground. His station wagon backed out of the driveway, smoke pouring out of the exhaust, the engine crackling. I watched the taillights grow smaller and smaller, until he took a right and disappeared.

A week later, Aunty Sue came back with a new Buddha. A month later, my mother signed the divorce papers like it was another bill. Almost a year later, I saw my father again as I was teeing off at the state sectional tournament in Deer Creek Country Club, the last golf tournament I would ever play. He stood along the fence, fingers through the chain link, a strong streak of white in his hair.

When I was six, my father took me to a palm reader in a seedy neighborhood in Chicago. He led me through a small alleyway and into a hidden apartment.

My father waited outside, not wanting to hear my future. I remember the palm reader, an elderly woman with thinning gray hair slicked back to hide a bald spot, had said red dots along the lifeline meant good fortune. A black dot signified bad luck. She tilted my hand in every angle, looking down her nose. Her skin felt so wrinkly and unpleasant, I wanted to yank my hand away and run out to my father. After ten minutes, the woman pointed to a black dot on my lifeline.

When I met my father, I was crying. Bad luck, I told him. I had bad luck because of a black dot. My father tried to calm me. He pulled me out of the alley and into the sun. He brought my hand out into the light. He looked closely at it. He saw the dot. He frowned. He scratched at it. He started laughing.

"Look," he said.

I looked and saw no black dot on my hand.

"Look," he said, wiggling a finger.

The black dot was on his finger.

"Safe," he said. He kissed the top of my forehead.

"What about my future?" I asked.

"Don't know," he said. "Maybe better not to."

Epilogue

Once there was a young prince, my mother would begin, who had the world in his pocket. If he wanted rice then a servant would crawl and deliver some to the feet of the prince. If he wanted to play soccer, then palace guards would round up boys from the village, and the prince would force the scared kids to play with him.

He wasn't a nice prince. In the market, they secretly sold a doll dressed in the prince's clothing, making it dance and contort in many unfavorable positions. Sometimes, after the sun had gone down, the villagers put on a play about the dumb prince and his selfishness. Usually, the play evoked so much laughter that the palace guards raided the performance and the villagers ran off, hoping to continue the next night.

The king and queen had no power over the prince, their son who brought the royal family shame.

"What do we do?" the king said.

"We spoil him," said the queen.

"Should we punish him?" the king said.

"We should," the queen said.

They tried, but the prince screamed so loud before a hand had even touched his bottom, the king and queen stopped, and showered the prince with kisses and apologies.

"We will get you a present," said the king.

"What would you like?" the queen said.

The prince took a moment to ponder. Finally, the prince said, "I want a white elephant. I want the great Iyala."

Such an impossible request! Iyala was practically a god. The great white beast had not been seen since the last war with Burma. A wise man said Iyala had flown to Heaven and was carrying Buddha on his back.

"This will be impossible," said the king.

"How about—" the queen said

"—just an elephant?" said the king.

The prince wailed and all the dogs in the village began to howl. "I want what I want!" he screamed.

"OK, OK," the king and queen agreed. "A white elephant. The great Iyala."

For months, no white elephant could be found, let alone Iyala. The king and queen sent their armies all over Siam. The king and queen tried to talk the spoiled prince into another present, perhaps a golden monkey, a white tiger from India, a bird of many colors that could talk. The prince said no to each alternate gift. "Iyala is what I want," he said. "Iyala is what I will get."

A year had passed, and it was magic that a white elephant happened to enter the palace walls undetected by the guards, feeding off the mangoes in the kingdom's orchard.

The king and queen rushed out into the orchard and bowed to the great beast as if it was Buddha himself.

"You have been searching for me?" said the great elephant, chewing slowly on mango.

"We have," said the king and queen.

The great elephant stood up on its hind legs; it was greater than the size of the tree. It picked the ripest mango on the tallest branch, snatching it easily with its enormous trunk.

"Your son shall have me for one week," said the elephant. "I will be what he wants, but be warned, this comes at price. If he does not change his ways, he will be taught a lesson."

The king and queen wanted to know what lesson. They wanted to ask. But the image of their son crying and shaking the palace walls with his wails made them hold their tongue. So instead, the king and queen shook the great elephant's trunk.

When Iyala was presented to the prince, the prince immediately climbed onto the great elephant's back and commanded him to do this and that.

"Walk through the village."

"Blow your trunk as loud as you can."

"Stand on one leg and hop."

Iyala did everything the prince commanded without complaint. "Anything you wish," the elephant said.

The prince loved Iyala, loved the power he had over the beast. But more than that, he loved when at night, the elephant slept at his side and warmed him with his breaths, loved that when he spoke the elephant listened attentively.

On the third day, it started to rain.

The prince, bored, whined incessantly. "When will this rain end?"

"Soon," said the elephant.

"But when is soon?" said the prince.

"When there is nothing more to cry about," said the elephant.

"I don't understand," said the prince.

"Patience," said the elephant.

After four days, the rain did stop, and the prince was so happy he kissed the elephant on the trunk. "The sun," shouted the prince. "Oh how I missed you." This joy had brought Iyala great comfort. Perhaps the prince had learned, had changed. "One more day," whispered the elephant.

Iyala and the prince strode off into the village. There was, however, no village to stride into. The rain had made a river and the village had been swept away. On the other side of the river, a woman was crying. Down the river a straw hat floated away.

The woman reached for the hat. "My baby," she said. "My baby."

The straw hat was not a straw hat after all, but a floating house, getting smaller and smaller until it became just a bobbing dot.

"What should we do?" said the elephant, leaving the decision to the prince, hoping he'd choose correctly.

The prince took a long time to think. Then he turned the other cheek and said, "Forget the woman. I am hungry. Take me to the orchard."

But the white elephant did not listen this time. He bucked the prince onto the ground and dove into the water, disappearing under its depth and reemerging hundreds of yards away. The elephant swam like a fish, his ears as oars paddled quickly. The prince screamed for the elephant to come back. The woman ran along the shore, clutching the air repeatedly as if trying to reel her baby to shore. Iyala reached the house. He pulled out an infant with his trunk, white wings grew out of his sides and he lifted off into the air. This great white beast was flying! He stopped in front of the woman and delivered the infant into her arms, who was fast asleep, soothed by the rocking river.

"Iyala," said the prince, "how dare you disobey me? You are my elephant."

The great beast checked the sun and realized a week had passed. He flew over to the boy, eyes red, smoke billowing out of his trunk.

"You have learned nothing," said the beast, in a voice so deep it shook the ground.

The prince had turned as white as the elephant's skin. He backed up against the wall.

"You will learn to respect, to love, to be a king." The great ivory tusk was aimed at the prince's throat. The prince began to cry; he cowered in the elephant's shadow.

The elephant stood on its hind legs and blew through its nose, so loud, so high-pitched, the prince covered his ears and the birds became silent. From the forest, the ground began to rumble, rhythmically, like footsteps. The leaves quivered. High above the tree line, a *yuk*, giant, galumphed toward Iyala and the prince. The giant's face was red, its nose had horns and its ears were wings.

The giant bowed to the elephant, then looked at the prince who was crying and screaming. The giant lifted the boy to its nose and smelled him. The boy covered his head with his arms. He rested in the palm of the giant's hand.

Iyala flew to speak into the giant's winged ear, in a language the boy did not understand. The giant grunted. Then, with a great swing of his massive arm, the giant propelled the boy into the air. The boy flew high and fast into clouds, into space, landing minutes later atop a mountain. He did not know where he was.

"Great elephant, I have learned," the boy cried. He was cold and alone. "Please come take me home. I am scared." But no one replied but the frosted wind.

Then in his ear, he heard Iyala: "When you get home you will be a man, ready to rule a kingdom. Find your way, and all will be right."

Before my American life began, I lay my head on my mother's lap, felt her hand rub my back as she spoke, and it was like that—lying in the shape of a cooked shrimp, my mother would say—that I drifted off to dreams of a fantastical world. This was my favorite of all her stories, the one I remember vividly over twenty years later. When telling the story, my mother sometimes added odd little details. The queen had freckles like her, the king had a large mole like my father, the rescued baby possessed shallow dimples like myself, and the air of this faraway land was like my aunt's aromatic garden.

In my imagination, I envisioned myself as the wise and magical white elephant Iyala, and those who came in and out of my life were characters in the tale—Mike transforming from an odd white boy into a *yuk* and Simon into the annoying prince. When I got older, it was not a baby that needed rescuing but my unrequited crushes, beautiful and wet and seductively flailing in the waters. Despite the changes, the story always ended the same way. The prince on the mountain. Cold and scared.

It didn't occur to me as a child that the ending of this story, a story my mother made up to answer my yearning for tales about Iyala, was particularly dark and frightening. I didn't identify with the prince, so it wasn't *me* left alone on that mountaintop. It was a story about the great white elephant, Iyala. It was a story about being a good person. But it was also a story about my family lost and alone in a foreign land, each of us on our own mountaintops, looking for some sign that would guide us home.

Over thirty years later, my mother and Aunty Sue finally found their way home. On July 18, 2004, the two boarded a plane in Chicago and flew twenty hours to Thailand. Now, when my mother calls to check in, her voice rings with happiness, without the weight that made her throat tight. She is home, and I wonder what she dreams about now.

Home—for me, for now—is not a place but that mysterious voice that beckoned to my mother in her dreams, the voice that still leads my father from one place to the next, the voice that never stops until you begin your journey.

The prince hears it. It is a constant buzz like a thirsty mosquito. He looks east, then west, but there is nothing but clouds and snow and rock. He wishes for foresight, to see beyond the extent of his eyes, but he knows his limitations. He knows if he stays on the mountain he will not survive. The first step, however, is the hardest. He lifts his foot, but yanks it back. He tries again with the same result. If only he knew which path would lead him home the quickest. If only he knew what dangers lurk ahead. He closes his eyes. He prays. His first step crunches the snow underneath him. He takes another step and another. The momentum of the mountain propels him forward until he is at a mad run. Running blindly. The wind rushes by. He doesn't feel the cold. Doesn't feel anything but the rush of the descent. He squeezes his eyes tighter. There is a moment where he trips over a rock and falls and tumbles down the mountain. He will trip and fall and tumble many times over. Each time, he will get up again and begin running. He won't open his eyes, no matter the temptation. Not for years. He will keep running. His lungs will fill with the air of anticipation. He will grow. He will mature. And when he is ready, he will open his eyes to see where his legs have led him.

About the Author

Katherine Riegel

Ira Sukrungruang has published fiction, nonfiction, and poetry in numerous periodicals and coedited *What Are You Looking At? The First Fat Fiction Anthology* and *Scoot Over, Skinny: The Fat Nonfiction Anthology.* He is Assistant Professor of English at the University of South Florida and lives in Brandon with his wife and three dogs.